LETTERS
FROM THE
BLITZ

LETTERS
FROM THE
BLITZ

TELLING AMERICA THE TRUTH ABOUT THE BRITISH EXPERIENCE OF WAR

RICHARD MacALPINE

The
History
Press

First published 2020

The History Press
97 St George's Place, Cheltenham,
Gloucestershire, GL50 3QB
www.thehistorypress.co.uk

British Library Cataloguing in Publication Data.
A catalogue record for this book is available from the British Library.

ISBN 978 0 7509 9429 3

Typesetting and origination by The History Press
Printed and bound in Great Britain by TJ International Ltd.

MIX
Paper from
responsible sources
FSC® C013056

CONTENTS

INTRODUCTION

On 1 September 1939 Hitler's armies crossed the border into Poland and set off a series of war declarations that resulted in the Second World War. Although the mood of the American public and Congress at that time was overwhelmingly isolationist, President Roosevelt could see the potential threat of Nazi Germany to the balance of power in Europe. As the German blitzkrieg rolled across Poland, Denmark, and the low countries, Roosevelt used his substantial political clout to convince a majority in Congress to scrap the earlier neutrality acts that included a total arms embargo and allow shipments of arms to America's old First World War allies, England and France, on a 'cash and carry' basis. That led to Germany's U-boat campaign in the Atlantic at substantial cost to American shipping. As the situation in Europe seriously eroded in the summer of 1940, with the fall of France and the withdrawal of British forces from Europe, the interventionists in Congress grew in power and influence. The isolationists in Congress objected vehemently to Roosevelt's executive order in August of 1940 which traded fifty old-age destroyers for the use of British bases in Canada and the Caribbean. As Britain stood alone against the onslaught of Nazi military power and withstood the bombing of British military facilities and cities in what became known as the Battle of Britain, President Roosevelt and the interventionists in Congress gained enough influence to pass the Lend Lease Act in March 1941 which basically gave the British the weapons they needed to defend themselves. That made the United States what Roosevelt called 'the arsenal of democracy'.

While the American Congress moved toward intervention in Europe, American public opinion did not. Instead the isolationist mood strengthened as conditions deteriorated in Europe. National hero Charles Lindbergh became the leading spokesman for the America First Committee and both toured the country and used the radio to tell the American people they were safe behind their oceans and if need be they could learn how to deal with Hitler. The war in Europe was not their fight. American public opinion was solidly isolationist until the morning of 7 December 1941. The Japanese changed everything that day.

It was that time period, 1939–42, that I was researching in my local newspaper here in Penn Yan, New York, the *Chronicle-Express*. I was preparing an article for our county history center's publication about how the attack on Pearl Harbor affected our community. I had previously seen letters published in the paper in the late 1930s by people with ties to our community who were either working or travelling in Germany. They wrote about various aspects of life under Nazi rule. There is a large Danish–American community in our area and when the Germans invaded Denmark there were letters in the *Chronicle-Express* written from Denmark about conditions there. Trying to maintain focus on the topic I was researching, I skimmed over those letters with the thought that I might refer back to them for future articles. As I got into the years 1940 and 1941, I noticed the occasional headline, 'Cousin In England Writes of Conflict and German Raids'. I finally decided to read one and it had a vivid description of the letter writer's thoughts on what became known as the 'miracle of Dunkirk'. A second one that I read described the writer undergoing training for fire control in Sheffield during the Battle of Britain. Another warned her cousin of the German propaganda machine that was spreading lies in America about how the British people were starving and their cities being totally destroyed. She advised her cousin to listen to the BBC for more accurate news.

From that point on, I shifted my focus to those letters. There was a lot of history in those letters and an important insight into the British spirit in the face of dire adversity. The letter writer was a woman named Winifred Graville who lived with her maid, Doris Hawkes, at 66 Ringinglow Road, less than 2 miles from the city centre of Sheffield, England (about 170 miles north of London). Miss Graville was in her mid-50s at the time and according to the *Chronicle-Express* was 'an authority on trees, flowers, and Old World gardens, having lectured and written widely on this interest'. She was a Fellow of the Royal Horticultural Society. According to the Bulletin of the Rotary Club of Sheffield, she was 'a born speaker with a lively sense of humour and of a ready wit. Miss Graville's reputation is such that the City of Sheffield has entrusted her with the creation of an Old World Garden, which will be one of the sights of the city.' Miss Graville's sense of humour and writing ability certainly came through in the letters that she wrote to America.

The recipient of the letters was Jane L. Beaumont of Penn Yan, New York. She was the wife of a prominent local businessman, insurance agent Charles Beaumont. Both were quite active in community affairs. At the time of the letters, Mrs Beaumont was the President of the Yates County Genealogical and Historical Society (a.k.a. the Yates County History Center). She and Winifred Graville were distant cousins with a mutual interest in genealogy who had connected years earlier through correspondence.

The first letter, although written on 5 October 1939, was not published in our local newspaper until 25 April 1940. From that point on, there were over 150 letters from Miss Graville published in our paper. The last one was written on 23 November 1942 but was not published until 21 January 1943. Jane Beaumont edited out the personal and family news before turning her cousin's letters over to the editor of the *Chronicle-Express*.

I pondered the question: Why were so many of these letters published in our local newspaper? Several times in the letters, Miss Graville voices her concern about the impact of German propaganda and misinformation and warns Americans not to accept it as true and accurate. It is obvious that the two cousins and the local editor were determined to, in a small way, educate the American people on the conditions in Britain and move them away from their isolationist attitude.

What they left us with is a wonderful, deeply personal, first-hand account of life in England during the dark early years of the Second World War, when Britain stood alone against the military might of Nazi Germany and the people made amazing sacrifices with an optimism and a spirit that was overwhelming, epitomising the message of 'Keep Calm and Carry On'. In one of the letters Miss Graville wrote:

> I don't want to grumble. I've made up my mind never to utter a grumble till the war is ended. As a woman whose home has been bombed to bits and had nothing but what she stood up in said: 'Well, we've got our lives – that to old 'Itler' and I'm afraid she made a rude face. The Germans may ruin our homes, bomb our beauty spots, and cause us some inconvenience, but they won't crush our spirits. It's born in us to be more determined than ever when we are wrongfully treated or up against things.

The true author of this book is Winifred Graville. My contribution is bringing her wonderful letters to light. Here they are presented exactly as they were published in the *Chronicle-Express* back in the 1940s. The researcher in me had the good fortune to stumble across her letters buried deep in our local newspapers from eighty years ago. The historian in me recognized the value of what was in them. I saw the patterns and the overall quality of her writing, transcribed the letters and added occasional notes to provide context. But it is her personality, descriptions, experiences and humour that makes this a worthwhile look at a critical period of British history. I would have liked to have known her.

Rich MacAlpine
Penn Yan, New York, USA

LETTERS FROM THE BLITZ

October 5, 1939

The war has very effectively stopped all lecturing in this country. I was hoping that my agent would arrange a lecture tour for me in America within the next year or two, but am much afraid that too will be stopped.

You folks, safe on the other side of the world, have no idea what it is like here. Not a streetlamp in Britain anywhere, not a light may show, even shops as well as private houses must present an absolutely black appearance from outside from sunset to sunrise. No chinks or faint glows, just utter blackness. Then too, every single person, children included, must by law carry their gas masks if more than five minutes away from home. Whenever I feel mine an awful nuisance, I just think perhaps some day I shall be only too thankful to wear it. As it is, I feel suffocated in it. I do not anticipate wearing it with any pleasure.

Unfortunately, Sheffield is one of the vulnerable areas. Thousands of children and mothers have been evacuated by the government or have taken themselves to country districts considered safer. Being out after dark is a real experience, for buses and trains are so darkened that you cannot recognize the person next to you and you cannot distinguish the money for your fare and as for crossing the streets, you hold your breath and bolt hoping for the best. Fortunately we have plenty of food, all of us, and there does not seem to be any likelihood of any shortage. I listen to the weekly broadcast from America by Raymond Gram Swing, though I do not know who he is or what position he holds in America.

Perhaps some day we may be able to meet, that is if the German aircraft are kept away from our country. Up to date we have not had a single air raid in Britain, our air force has chased them off every time. Even an optimist cannot expect that to happen indefinitely. This country has been flooded with refugees of all nationalities. I am afraid the poor things may have to suffer again, if luck favors the German aircraft at any time.

November 4, 1939

The weather has been very foggy with torrential rains. We are very tired of it, but feel secure from air raids with the fog. The last two nights I looked out of the door on my way up to bed and I literally could not see the door step although I was standing on it. I do not remember such darkness, but we are thankful for it. It is protection.

Sheffield is an armament city – armor plates, shells, steel plates for the battleships and submarines etc. are all made here. We are built on hills and all around and in the city are anti-aircraft guns. If we know where they are, we are asked not to tell even our best friends, as there are spies here. They will get them sooner or later we know, but they can be very dangerous. For instance, there are about 100 to 200 air balloons round the very dangerous works and one day they were taken down (for inspection, I believe) and that afternoon Germany broadcast in English saying that they knew our balloons were down and mentioned a gas decontamination centre recently made in a residential area and one or two of the big works by name, saying they would shortly be bombed.

Those of us who live close to anti-aircraft guns have been told when they are firing during a bombardment, that we are to lie down flat, face downwards, on the floor with our mouths wide open and our ears stopped up, if there's time to get cotton wool. If not, cover them tightly with our hands in order that our ear drums will not burst with the concussion etc. A friend who lives in a block of flats opposite a barracks has been ordered to board up all windows for the duration of the war. The tenants of the flats have to pay for it themselves. It looks dreadful. All the shops underneath boarded up too.

If you want to get authentic news, listen in (if your set is powerful enough) to the BBC news at 9 o'clock every night. The *Ark Royal*, the *Repulse*, and the *Iron Duke* are not sunk up to date in spite of anything the Germans may say. We are not starving yet either and there are no food queues. We are to be rationed with butter and bacon, but most of those two supplies come from abroad and will not store. We are compelled by law to carry our gas masks and wear identification disks. All over the city every few yards air raid shelters have been made for our safety, if caught when out from home. They are underground, made of concrete and very cold. I dread having to rush into one. I just hate to see children carrying gas masks. The little mites ought not to know the horrors of war. Thousands of people have shut up their houses and gone into the country for the duration. Only those whose work keeps them or those who cannot afford to leave are staying here.

I have just had a 'gas mask' made for my canary. He is a very great pet. The 'gas mask' is a large glass jar with a screw top and the sort of stuff our masks are composed of fitted into the top so that the air will be freed from poison before he breathes it. I don't want even a little canary to die in agony with poison gas if I can prevent it. Frankly, I dread gas attacks far more than ordinary air raids. I feel suffocated in the mask, though the doctors fitted mine properly and inspected it a week or two ago to see that it was still functioning all right. I don't know what anyone would do who had a cold in the head!

I forgot to mention about the wireless news — that there is a German broadcast every night in perfect English, pretending to be

London and giving the most awful lies as news. It says terrible things about England and the British. We all put it on so as to have a good laugh. We don't mind a bit. The news is really intended for Americans and other gullible neutrals. Though no one in Europe believes a single word that comes from anybody in Germany, it might impress people who do not know that it is not really English.

November 8, 1939

The peace project of Belgium and Holland sounds all right on paper. The fact is however, that they are scared to death of Hitler and who can blame them? There can be no peace with the Nazis. They have broken their word too often. So I am afraid it will not come to anything. Hitler would like it. He has been declaring that the British navy has been swept from the seas and then goes on to say: 'Britain cannot be allowed to be the dictator of the seas.' The two statements, like many of his, do not fit.

December 9, 1939

Did you see the King and Queen when they were in the USA? They are idolized over here. She is tremendously popular in all classes of the community. She broadcast to the women of the empire a week or two ago, a simple, homely, moving little speech delivered in a quiet, clear voice. Sundry working women have said to me: 'She might have been an ordinary woman in an ordinary house like this.'

The war goes on, getting more and more terrible, but our anti-aircraft force is wonderful and up to now the German air force has never penetrated inland. In many cases, they never even reach the coast. A girl was telling me about her mother, who lives 15 miles in from the coast of Yorkshire. Some German mines washed ashore all those miles away and every window in her village was smashed with the explosion. Her father has started to keep fowls. He has two black cockerels which he has named Hitler and Stalin. None of the hens will have Hitler anywhere near them!

December 12, 1939

The *New York Times* made me very cross reporting that four of our fleet had been sunk by German aircraft. Up to the time of this writing, their aircraft has never managed to hit any ships at all. Nor have their bombers ever got through our coastal defenses. Not yet. But at the rate they fly now, we are about eight minutes flight from the coast. So by the time you receive this, U-boats and mines permitting, we may have had a horrid time. But I have great faith in our air defenses.

December 28, 1939

A neighbour was very interested in the picture in the *Rochester Times Union* of the British aircraft sinking the submarine. Such pictures are not allowed in our newspapers. Next week we shall be rationed for butter and bacon. We are allowed four ounces butter per person per week. As I easily eat eight ounces, I'm going to have to scrape (literally.) One of my friend's brothers is going to get me two pounds next week.

January 7, 1940

The Germans broadcast quite frequently that their planes have been over Britain. Up to the time of writing, no enemy plane has penetrated our defenses. They have all either been met in the North Sea and driven off or else they have been shot down at the coast. This makes quite a number of people think we are safe from attack always, but sensible folks know only too well that state of affairs is hardly likely to last until the end of the war. Some planes are bound to get through at some time. They may get into Britain, but they are very unlikely to get out again! Besides, once they begin bombing civilians the Germans will have to have a taste of their own tactics.

Tomorrow we begin rationing three-quarters pound sugar, four ounces butter, and six ounces bacon each. The maid and I will have one-half pound of bacon for breakfast per week between us instead of our usual two pounds! I am not complaining – no one complains – but what is one to eat?

We have had very keen frosts and thick fogs for almost a fortnight. The sun came out for about half an hour this afternoon and now the fog is as thick as ever. It spells safety from air raids but, oh dear, it does make things so black!

Today at midday we were told by BBC news that enemy planes penetrated over the Yorkshire cliffs, so they were not very far away. Anyhow, they were driven off without doing us much damage. They were also over Thames estuary, Newcastle, Firth of Forth, and Norfolk coast. They are beginning on us at last. Yesterday a.m. I was at work in my study enjoying the bright sunshine which was flooding the room, when I suddenly heard the sirens – air raid warning! I jumped up and looked out of the windows and a friendly van driver called out: 'Don't be alarmed. It's only practice!' I had completely forgotten they were practicing all over Yorkshire to see if the sirens and equipment were all in working order. The siren quite close to this house is awful. You can have no conception what it sounds like. The wailing of the damned in torture is an angelic choir compared to 'Wailing Willie' as I have named it. It's awful going up and down, makes you go cold through and through. Your stomach drops down and your heart jumps up and your legs feel like daisy stalks. After a few minutes you are able to walk about, but feel like an empty cocoon when the insect has left it.

Each night when we go to bed, we fill the kettle with water. We are not allowed to draw water during an air raid in case of poisoned water. Set a little tray with teapot and cups and saucers, leave a candle and matches in readiness in case all electricity has gone. Upstairs we place a thick, warm coat and frock together with our gas masks where we can find them without delay in the dark. I always have my handbag with the door key and my money in it. No one knows what they might have to do and if we had to run out of the house because it was being bombed. I might as well take such money I possessed with me!!!

Yesterday I sent off two local newspapers which gave descriptions of the bombing and machine gunning of fishermen trying to get into their lifeboats after the vessels had been sunk – barbarous and disgusting behaviour. What a day of reckoning awaits the German nation! I only hope they won't destroy all our vegetation with poisonous gases. Apart from the loss of crops, we do not want our gardens, nor 'England's green and pleasant land' utterly ruined beyond redemption.

January 30, 1940

The snow in the garden is four feet deep. Thousands of folk had no milk or newspapers yesterday. The country is having the worst weather since 1869 – in Sheffield the keenest frost ever known. Nine out of ten houses have no water. Traffic everywhere is disorganized. Yesterday we had no bread or newspapers. I have not had my *Sunday Times* yet and it is Tuesday! Many main lines on the railway are blocked with snow. Everything is very bad connected with transport. The Germans somehow know. Yesterday they attacked the whole of the coast from Shetlands down to the English Channel at 9 a.m. all at once. Not one broke through our defenses! So they bombed and machine gunned ships that were unprotected, that is had no guns on board and there were some sad homes as a result. As soon as our aircraft come to grips with them, they turn tail and scatter off to Germany as fast as they can.

The maid is going out bread hunting, as my baker for some reason unknown to me is unable to deliver up here. Although I rang him up and 'said a few words.' So I will bring this to a close and she will post it for me.

March 5, 1940

I am wondering what Mr. Sumner Welles (Under Secretary of State) will say to America when he gets back. I cannot think that an astute people like the Americans will put much faith in any of Hitler's peace proposals.

What I tell you about conditions here are absolutely true and there are some things I'd love to tell, but we are asked to be most careful, as information of no seeming value might be very useful if it fell into enemy hands. We have been asked to let friends and relatives abroad know how we are going on, as in some parts of the world there is great anxiety about friends in Britain owing to the exaggerated broadcasts of the Nazis. Their bombers have been very active off the east coast. A girl was telling me this a.m. that she had just come back from the Yorkshire coast (her home) and was having tea in a house overlooking the bay of a famous watering place, when they saw two of our destroyers and German aircraft having a battle. Everyone seized coat and ran out to watch. The Germans didn't hit anything more than the sea and when our airmen arrived on the scene they turned tail and flew back as usual with everyone on the front cheering like mad!! Many dead bodies have been washed up on the coast and the undertaker told the girl's father that the skipper of a fishing vessel had been so badly hit with machine gun bullets that his body was like a sieve. He had hardly been able to prepare the poor fellow's body for burial, so riddled with holes was his corpse. The fishing vessel did not happen to be armed, so they could not protect themselves. Who would want to be governed by people who could behave like that to innocent unarmed folk pursuing their daily occupations as usual? The lifeboat went out to the rescue of some men who had their ship torpedoed under them and the Germans bombed and sank the lifeboat.

There are no food queues and there is no food shortage and up to the moment of writing, no enemy aircraft has got into England. The one brought down at Whitby (Yorkshire) was of course at the coast. There is plenty of food though not always of the kind one usually prefers. The alleged lamb that we had at the weekend was I am sure the identical ram that accompanied Noah on his cruise on the Ark and I am wondering if after hours of stewing once more, it will be less like India rubber than it was when we tried to eat it on Saturday! Tho' in all fairness, I am bound to admit that our meat is not usually so tough.

I too wish the war was over, but I am afraid there are some very bad times ahead for all concerned and I am quite sure it will spread and that there will be neutral countries who have to come in out of self-protection. The Nazis will stop at nothing to gain their own ends.

How lovely to be free from food rationing, blackouts, scarcity of some of the things one loves and is used to, but that are not strictly necessary such as flowers, beautiful colours in materials, paper, etc. and above all the ever lasting uncertainty whether one will be alive even in a few hours time. The nuisance of carrying one's gas mask if one is going more than five minutes away from home. The restriction of all forms of transport, the need for care in one's speech about friends serving with the forces. This England of ours was once the Home of the Free. It is still and always will be and every one of us is absolutely willing to do all we can to ensure that freedom. We grumble, of course we do, we shouldn't be British if we didn't. We find fault with our leaders, both national and civic. Why shouldn't we? Our music hall comedians make great fun of Mr. Chamberlain's umbrella, Winston Churchill's hat, Lord Halifax's rationing, air raid shelters and the blackout and everybody roars with laughter and nobody bothers about their dignity. All the inconveniences to which we are subjected are the cause of fun, but underneath it all, we are determined to see it through. That does not mean that we are not very anxious and worried, but it does mean we are not going to give in.

March 16, 1940

Meat rationing came in last Monday. You can tell men are at the head of affairs, for instead of allowing us so much weight per head, they are allowing each person one-tenth per head per week. Everyone is racing for the cheap cuts and the better meat is not so popular. My normal meat bill for one week is seven-sixths at cost. My maid and I together are now allowed three-eighths per week. I have eaten so much mutton lately that I feel like baaa-ing. But I shall not grumble at the butcher, poor man, he is having a hard time.

Every newspaper and magazine you send me are passed on and eagerly read by a number of folk who are eager to know America's point of view. My young doctor in France wrote that he had been slow in acknowledging the last lot I sent him because six of his men had been doing a very unpatriotic thing, having German measles.

NOTE: *In another letter written in March, Miss Graville reported that she had met a William Millspaugh, who had been raised in Branchport (near her cousin's home in Penn Yan) and attended the early years of Keuka College. His father was Levi Millspaugh, who ran a wagon shop in Branchport for years and whose house on the lake later became Chateau Dugas. William Millspaugh, a mechanical engineer who got his start in industry in Ohio, between 1933 and 1948 owned a foundry in England (Millspaugh Ltd of Sheffield) that made castings in steel and bronze. He lived with his daughter and her husband not far from Miss Graville.*

May 10, 1940

Mr. William Millspaugh called to see me one night and told me a good deal about Penn Yan and America. He seems to be a wonderful man for his age. He was very interesting about conditions in western Europe, concerning business and the lives of the people. He has personal friends in several of the now warring countries. But I think his favourite is Norway. He told me a good deal about America. Apparently there is little to choose between the poverty of Britain or America. He told me I should see a great difference in some of the places in the US after having lived in the fifth largest city in the kingdom. I told him I hoped I should not meet any pro-Germans over there for the fur would fly!!! He thinks England a lovely country to live in. He was delighted that I sent him the article by Verdi Burtch (of Branchport) and he told me of some of their boyhood times. He drew me a plan of your lake. (I can't spell it without looking at the map.)

The news this a.m. is dreadful. I have been wandering around the garden looking for buds and shoots to try to cheer myself up. Poor Europe to be at the mercy of such an evil gang as Hitler & Co.

NOTE: *After what had been a seven-month 'Phoney War' with very little activity in Western Europe, the German Army and Air Force began a six-week campaign on 10 May which would end with the surrender of the Netherlands, Belgium, Luxembourg and, in June, France. Also on 10 May, British Prime Minister Neville Chamberlain resigned and was quickly succeeded by Winston Churchill.*

May 12, 1940

Your letter was so nice to get just after all the dreadful war news. I had been awake all night listening to the drone of airplanes overhead.

Our folk were watching and guarding us carefully, but I wish they were not quite so noisy about it. Up to the moment of writing our rations are still the same, but we may have butter and bacon reduced.

During the week I saw a military convoy pass. I had better not say where. It took nearly two hours to pass. I realized what a mechanized thing war is today. There were numbers of what I took to be anti-aircraft guns, very long and slim, every one with names painted on what Doris would call 'the spout' and I said I thought that was the barrel, tho' I may be wrong too!! Some humorist had been busy. I cannot remember them all, but some stuck in my mind. 'Hell Fire', 'Suicide Pal', 'Calamity Jane' (I regret a number of them bore feminine names). 'The Avenger' sounded too much like a warship, but who on Earth was 'Tony de Wop?' They had their mouths tied up with red flannel for all the world as if they were suffering from toothache. The camouflage on the military wagons was wonderful and the soldiers' 'tin hats' looked as if they would do with a good polish. The tin hat of one of the officers looked as tho' he'd been white washing in it! The cars of the staff officers looked like poultry vans tacked onto ordinary car engines. Mere lieutenants rode in the vans with the men. There were funny little cars like water beetles and scores of motorcycle dispatch riders, some of them with maps fastened onto their handlebars and others with big white boards across their chests. Vans full of the weirdest instruments. I cannot imagine what they were for! Bren guns, which in my ignorance I mistook for tanks and which made you feel seasick to watch cavorting up the road for all the world like nervous hunting horses anxious to take off. Goodness knows where they were going to. I felt safer from parachute troops after I had seen them, for I am only 45 minutes walk from the great stretches of moorlands and parachutists might try to land there.

We were very upset over the manner of Mr. Chamberlain's resignation. The country as a whole was deeply ashamed of the abominable treatment of the Labour parties to a man who is a gentleman in the true sense of the word and who had been a fine leader. If it was necessary to change leaders – and some thought so who were of Mr. Chamberlain's own party – he should have been told in a more kindly and courteous manner. The country was disgusted. Mr. Chamberlain, brave old man, announced his own resignation over the wireless in a dignified speech without any bitterness or reproach, though you could tell it was emotional and appealed for loyal support for Winston Churchill. The very fact that the Nazis loathe Mr. Churchill so, shows that they are afraid of him. The Germans cannot learn that however much we quarrel amongst ourselves, we are united against them!

I wonder what Italy will do. It will be suicidal for her to go in with Germany as the Abyssinians will rise up at once and we will then have the Italians bottled up in the Mediterranean. This war ought surely to be a strong warning to all countries never to submit to a dictator. In countries under dictators there is no liberty of thought, action, or even of soul. Hitler has stated he is to be King of England, emperor of India, Canada, Australia, and ruler of Europe. He will never be King of England anyway because the British have been free too long to put up with dictators dictating! The row in our House of Commons could not have happened in any country under a dictator. Under a dictatorship, the same feelings might be felt and would smolder underneath causing a hidden fire to break forth some day in a manner horrible to think of. As it is, in Britain we had the row, the change was made. It is over, we are now carrying on as usual. In a few days, all unpleasantness will be forgotten and no lives lost over it.

Such lots of people stop to admire the front garden. At present there is a border the whole way round and round the inner rose bed of blue forget-me-nots. These flowers, along with primroses, always have a special appeal for Britons. There is also a lovely yellow azalea out, covered with richly scented flowers, as it is next to a silvery grey leaved shrub. The colour scheme is very lovely and seems to be appreciated by passersby. The copper beech by the gate is also out and its young foliage is glorious. When I look out the window and view my handiwork (greatly assisted by nature) I feel the world to be a lovely place. Even Hitler and his evil gang are temporarily forgotten.

We have got so many balloons up now that they are almost as thick in the sky as stars. There is only one direction free from them and as I love sky and clouds, I look that way most often.

I enclose a snapshot of myself in my gas mask. If you look at it through a magnifying glass, you will see how terrible it looks. I can assure you it feels 50 times worse than it looks.

It is impossible to find out when the mails are leaving for the US. If the post office authorities know, they will not say. So I just have to hope I'm lucky and then in about a fortnight's time after posting, I try to picture you receiving my epistles and hope that you have sufficient time to read them!

Did I tell you that everything you send in the way of mags and papers are passed on to many folk? I have today sent *Time* to my doctor's brother, a major in the RAMC (Royal Army Medical Corps.) The doctor called this a.m. to see me. They are rather anxious about him. He was home on a leave a fortnight ago and told us he was stationed in the very front line of the Franco–Belgian–German front. He said he wished something would happen. He will have had his wish 'ere now and, as the Germans have bombed a military hospital and fired on doctors, nurses, and wounded alike, we are wondering about him. I spent all yesterday sitting quietly reading as I was too poorly to do anything else. Your papers were a godsend. All ours, even the mags, are full of war.

I have always wished I lived further out on the moors. Now I am glad I do not. It seems parachutists are a real danger. But I'm not too nervous, as we are ready and waiting. But the moon is rising and we may expect them any night now. Sheffield is one of the places they are anxious to reach and South Yorkshire is the place they have to land. By the time you receive this, goodness knows what the evil beasts will have done.

May 16, 1940

Did I tell you I have a book nearly completed of flower arrangements with my own illustrations – photography? I am wanting to try USA with it. Nothing doing here at all in that line at present. Won't be till all this awful slaughter is over.

Am disgusted with Queen Wilhelmina (Netherlands), after all she said to us about not wanting our help. Then she and all the lot of them come chasing over here. Good old King Haakon and Prince Olaf didn't leave Norway.

May 19, 1940

It has been a terribly anxious week. The war is so wickedly pursued by the Germans. It seems like devilry let loose. Even many British feel that now the only way to teach the brutes a lesson is to bomb Berlin until not one stone is left on another like they did in Poland. If fate decreed that they should win – and no one here believes or intends that they should – the world would be given over to bestiality, oppression, and misery worse than anything in the Middle Ages.

Anthony Eden broadcast an appeal for volunteers to cope with the parachutist troops. Before he had finished, men of all ages were besieging the police stations etc. anxious to defend the country from that awful menace. It is just the sort of thing young men the world over would enjoy. A young neighbour of mine studying at the University to be a dentist told me they have formed defense corps to guard the University itself for reasons anyone can guess for themselves.

I am sitting in the garden in blazing sunshine with flowers all around me – mostly forget-me-nots. The sky is absolutely cloudless and for the moment, there are no balloons up to remind us of the awful struggle going on in the continent and which any minute may be brought here.

Britain is proud of the navy again this week. I have been wondering very much if J.M. has been taking part. If he has, he won't be allowed to say. I am worried about my Dr's. brother. A fortnight ago he said as he went down my path to his car after a short visit: 'I wish something would happen.' I said: 'But you are safe while it is like this.' He replied: 'But it's been so boring, eight months of doing nothing. I might as well have been at home looking after my patients.' We are all wondering very much if he is one of the doctors deliberately bombed by the Germans as they make definite attacks on hospitals, ambulances, and Red Cross units. His mother called to see me yesterday and is very worried. We are all telling her no news is good news. I think she knows perfectly well that we do not really think so in this case, any more than she does.

Another friend is in a state about her only son who went to Norway in the beginning and they've never heard a word since. Isn't it dreadful? Why can't everyone live in peace and security? Why should there be all this suffering? And all through the insatiable greed and bumptiousness of one apology for a man. I should not envy him in the hereafter throughout eternity.

NOTE: *Between this letter and the next one, the German Army overran the Netherlands, Belgium and most of France. Most of the British Army along with thousands of their French and Belgian allies were trapped with their backs to the sea along the northern French coast at Dunkirk. Inexplicably, the German High Command approved orders to halt the offensive just short of Dunkirk. That allowed what became known as the 'Miracle of Dunkirk', as over 300,000 troops were evacuated to England from the beaches by large ships, small pleasure craft and fishing vessels. The evacuation started on 26 May and was completed by 4 June.*

Richard MacAlpine

May 31, 1940

Since I wrote last, what a lot has happened. To think that less than a month ago the Belgian king appealed to us and the French for help and then without a word to either and against the advice and wishes of his own government, he capitulates leaving thousands of British and French troops trapped. Such treachery is inconceivable. Most people are now inclined to the belief that he did it by previous arrangement with Hitler and Mussolini. Now that we are in a tight corner, Mussolini is apparently going to kick us too!

The British and French navy are being absolutely splendid. They have got thousands of French and British and Belgians safely away into England. Poor gallant little Belgium! We understand they have deposed the king and intend to fight on. We are very indignant with Holland and that autocratic old lady who sits on the Dutch throne. Before the invasion of Holland she told us repeatedly that she did not need our help, that the Dutch could look after themselves and their colonies. Then after a few days of invasion she gave in, though our troops were warned. At least the Dutch did not have us trapped. Now they are only too thankful to accept our guardianship of their colonies and Queen Wilhelmina herself was found wandering about on the quayside looking for a ship to bring her to England. A naval officer found her and brought her with her daughter and son-in-law and baby to these shores. She broadcast to us and made speeches but unlike any of the other suffering nations, she has never uttered, publicly at any rate, one word of thanks for what has been done for them. Hitler was trying to take her prisoner too!

We are terribly anxious about our doctor's brother, but yesterday he sent a telegraph to say that he was safe in England. We are glad to know of the safety of our friends, but we think of those who will not come, but whose graves will be a lasting memorial of the treachery of a Belgian king whose own father fought to the finish

26 years ago and who will go down in history as one of the noble men of Europe. His son's name will be execrated by decent men and women for all time.

J.M. was home on short leave this week and came to see me. I am very sorry to find that he has been slightly shell shocked and wounded in the foot. He took part in the evacuation of troops from Holland, as the Germans were entering the town only a few hundred yards away. The sailors had the time of their lives and couldn't help laughing at the description of the demolition parties. Sailors who had never driven motor cars in their lives, all piling in until the bottom nearly dropped out! Driving or cavorting about till they could upset it in an awkward place and fire it. All the residents had left and our sailors blew up the docks, harbor, bridges, dykes, roads – everything they could. They had to wait till the last soldier was over, the Germans close behind, fuse the bridges with quick time explosives or hand bombs and run for it – all under heavy fire from the German's heavy guns and bombing from the air. They were nearly home when they were attacked from the air. They got home, but he would say so little about the attack and shuddered when I mentioned bombing. I asked if there were any wounded, but he looked so upset and said: 'Oh! Don't.' I can only conclude that he saw ghastly scenes and the shell shock he is suffering from keeps him from forgetting. He doesn't seem able to throw it off. I took him to the theater to see J.M. Barrie's play, *What Every Woman Knows*. He did enjoy it. It would do him good and help him forget the war. It is sad to see such a nice fellow, strong and healthy, so nerve wracked.

NOTE: *There are a number of references in these letters to 'J.M.' He may be a neighbour or a relative, but it is never made clear in Miss Graville's letters. They were regular correspondents. As the Netherlands was overrun by the Germans in May 1940, the British Navy sent demolition squads into the ports to destroy the facilities there. J.M. was apparently part of that.*

Some of the soldiers back from Norway and Belgium are very nerve wracked. They were a great deal more upset over the plight of the refugees and the cruelty and barbaric treatment of women and children than they were over their own wounds. A woman of my acquaintance was talking to a young soldier back from Norway. We had all seen an account in the newspaper of the Germans having shot some children playing in a field. This boy was there and said that they (the British) had refrained from shooting on account of the children, but the second the kiddies were shot, some older soldiers who were there were up and over the walls before the young men had time to wink, after the Germans. The young men collected themselves and in spite of the hail of bullets, they reached those evil beasts, none of whom will harm anyone again. The returned men say that the devils deliberately drive the tanks over exhausted refugees lying in the road and regularly machine gun women and children.

Well, now we are told it is our turn. We do not believe there will be an invasion from the sea, but parachutist troops appear to be a real menace and, of course, we know what to expect from air attacks. It is dreadful to think that civilization seems to be returning to brute force and that clever brains are thinking out methods of destruction instead of means to reduce suffering and poverty.

Our gas masks have had another respirator added to the end on account of another gas the Germans intend to use. They are very heavy and no nicer to wear then they were. Up to now Hitler and his evil gang have used no gas. But we know it has been reserved for us and every kind of devilry that vile minds can conceive.

Our sugar ration has been reduced to one half pound per head. Just when the doctor has ordered me to eat quantities of it too! The butter is to be one-fourth per head instead of one half pound each. We are still not short of food, but there are thousands of refugees and prisoners to feed as well as ourselves. I have often thought Britain has ever been the refuge of persecuted nations of the world, but where would the British themselves find refuge should such a horrible necessity arise? There would be nowhere. They would just kill us all. I must not dwell on thoughts like that. I am not a 'Dismal Jimmy' but I know we are up against an unscrupulous, evil foe who will never hesitate to use the most cruel means to gain his own end. Yes, he may try, but right always triumphs in the end.

> **NOTE:** *One needs to remember the old adage that truth is the first casualty of war. Although the Germans were certainly guilty of propagandising with exaggerations, falsehoods and misinformation, so too was the BBC.*

June 1, 1940

We have all been tremendously stirred by the landing in England of the French, Belgian, and British troops trapped in Belgium. The navies and our air force have done marvelous work. But, oh, those poor men. The first batch that arrived here in Sheffield came just as they were. There was no time for first aid or anything. They were picked up and rushed off to the coast and brought before the unwounded. Poor fellows, covered with dirt and blood, in tattered uniforms, they poured into this country and doctors and nurses worked frantically to save them. Then the evacuation of the others began. Meanwhile the Germans, with characteristic brutality, sank two hospital ships. These vessels were painted white and clearly marked with the Red Cross, but they deliberately bombed them both until they sunk. (I should think the very word 'German' will stink in the nostrils of decent people the world over.)

Britain is all along receiving the soldiers from plucky little Belgium. As the troop trains pass the country stations and level crossings, our people are there to give them hot tea, buns, cigarettes, postcards for them to write to their relatives and do any mortal thing they can. The Belgians and French who can speak no English smile and say: 'Vive le Angleterre' and shake hands violently to express their gratitude. Many men are so exhausted that they drop fast asleep as soon as they sit down. Some are lame, never having had their boots off for nearly a week and many of them are soaking wet, having been obliged to wade up to their necks in water in order to reach the vessels waiting to bring them home, all the time under heavy aerial bombardment. A porter at one of the stations said to one of the wet soldiers: 'Well, chum, have you had a good time?' and received the reply: 'I've ruddy well learned to swim, mate.' (only he used a more gory word than ruddy!) Everyone is full of admiration for little Belgium. But what of its king? He has lost his throne as well as his honor. I wonder what will happen to him.

The Germans have left their own wounded to die without making any attempt to tend to them. The dead are piled up in thousands. It is to be hoped that some horrible epidemic will not break out and sweep across Europe. If it did, it might do away with Nazism and all the cruelty and oppression that it stands for, but unfortunately innocent folks would suffer too, like they always do.

All aliens, whether friendly or otherwise, are now being interned. There has been so much treachery in other countries through the 'fifth column' that our leaders are running no risks. Of course, they are being very comfortably housed and properly fed, etc. so I think most of them realize our necessity for caution and will not mind unduly.

We are quite ready for the parachutists, too. Britain has had time to profit from the misfortunes of some of the other countries and our new coalition government is going ahead with munitions and preparations for any contingency. By the way, if you should happen to hear a new station calling itself 'The New British Broadcasting Station', beware. It is another of the enemy stunts and is not British nor authentic.

June 2, 1940

One of your newspapers prints a list of warships, destroyers and other war vessels that the Germans claim to have sunk. Surely Americans take any German statements with a teaspoonful, not a pinch, of salt. We were told by the Ministry of Information the other night that the Germans claim to have sunk 25 more capital ships than we possessed at the beginning of the war. They do not admit to the world that they lost a third of their navy over the Norwegian affair.

The French and British navy together with trawlers, sailing vessels, pleasure boats, anything that can be used at all, are fetching the men away in thousands. Ought they to be left to be murdered, for the Germans could not feed them if they took them prisoners? No! The withdrawal will go down in history as one of the most wonderful feats ever known to the world. I wish all America could know about it. Each vessel had 20 bombing planes try to attack it. Our aircraft were marvelous, and a sailor said to me: 'You folks at home have no idea what you owe to the aircraft.' Everyone that could do anything did it. A boy of 15 crossed backwards and forwards without ceasing with his father in a fishing cobble for three days and nights, loading the boat to the bursting point fetching away the soldiers – French, Belgian, and English. Every one of them is utterly exhausted and all they want is a good wash and a sleep. Lord Gort (commander of British forces) was on the beach with them, absolutely refusing to leave till he had seen his men safe onboard for 'England, home, and beauty' (and sleep.) However, the government and the king ordered him to leave at once. Being a good soldier, he obeyed orders, but he declined to travel with any pomp and ceremony. I believe he crossed on a little boat and landed right away from crowds. He was met in London by Mr. Anthony Eden and one or two others. It was mainly because Mr. Eden was there that the people on the station realized someone important was arriving and he was only recognized by a few. He is a quiet, unassuming man with no fuss about him. Not for him armored trains and motor cars, no bulletproof suits, nor streets lined with soldiers at attention, no bombastic boasting like his opponent, the Fuhrer, except when he merely wipes his nose in public. The British army adores Lord Gort to a man, they would follow him anywhere.

It was a tremendous relief to England to hear that they got practically the whole of the trapped armies out of Flanders by midnight last night and I think they will finish the work very soon now. The British navy says it has been like serving on pleasure boats going from Blackpool to the Isle of Man in the season with trippers! Except of course for the horrible bombing. They just simply loaded up and left at once and the next one slipped in, loaded up, went and was followed by another and so on, always pursued by heavy firing and terrific air attacks and torpedo boats, etc. All the men say: 'All we want is a good sleep and then we'll meet old Hitler again.'

Bartimaeur, a famous naval author, broadcast description of the beach at Dunkirk and the work of the navy and of every conceivable kind of vessel that could float. Some of the men and lads of seventeen joined in the rescue work, had never seen a bomb in their lives, but they just carried on. The sea, too, behaved itself so that small craft could cross. Last Sunday was a day of national prayer. The faith of many was shaken when we heard of the king of the Belgians dreadful decision on Tuesday a.m., but when we learned of the well nigh impossible rescue of all those trapped armies, many a prayer of thankfulness was offered for their safety.

After all the awful loss of life and utter destruction of several countries, what has Hitler gained? In Holland the farmland was flooded and the coastal towns flooded and absolutely demolished by the request of the Dutch themselves to our navy. The harbors and aerodromes ruined. In Belgium coal mines flooded, aerodromes and coastal towns flooded and blown to bits. In Stavanger, Norway the aerodrome is mostly useless to them owing to our ceaseless attacks from the air. At sea he is powerless to do much, in Germany they are short of food. The supplies in Denmark did not last long, so the Nazis rationed the country they had entered to 'protect' so that the people themselves are suffering hardships there, as in Norway, Holland, and Belgium.

Well, we are awaiting the next round with confidence, knowing that we are in for a bad time. But nothing we can suffer here will be equal to what the men in Flanders and the navies and boats of all kinds that went to their aid went through. By the time this reaches you, I hope it will, there is no knowing what we shall have encountered. But don't let anyone in America think we are starving or anywhere near it. We are not and all Britain is determined to endure what comes, so that the cruel regime of the Nazis may be overthrown.

It is difficult at times to imagine such horrors as are happening every moment elsewhere. For spring has come. There is nothing on earth quite like an English spring. The cuckoo is calling all day long and birds are busy singing everywhere. Last week, BBC broadcast Bird Song From A Surrey Wood and we listened to the voices of all kinds of birds singing as if in a contest to see which of them could sing the loudest! The trees are fully covered with their flowers and leaves. Gardens are becoming gay and the woods are carpeted with bluebells, that misty mauve blue which no artist can ever paint correctly.

NOTE: In June 1940, France, Hitler's last remaining opponent in Western Europe, was facing certain defeat. On 4 June, Prime Minister Churchill, in a famous speech to the House of Commons, said:

Even though large tracts of Europe and many old and famous States have fallen or may fall into the grip of the Gestapo and all the odious apparatus of Nazi rule, we shall not flag or fail. We shall go on to the end. We shall fight in France, we shall fight on the seas and oceans, we shall fight with growing confidence and growing strength in the air, we shall defend our island, whatever the cost may be. We shall fight on the beaches, we shall fight on the landing grounds, we shall fight in the fields and in the streets, we shall fight in the hills; we shall never surrender, and if, which I do not for a moment believe, this island or a large part of it were subjugated and starving, then our Empire beyond the seas, armed and guarded by the British Fleet, would carry on the struggle, until, in God's good time, the New World, with all its power and might, steps forth to the rescue and the liberation of the old.

June 7, 1940

Doris (my maid) and I are now, at 1:45 a.m., sitting downstairs after a sudden horrible wailing from 'Willie'. Hitler has started on us in earnest at last. Undoing the bolts of the front door in case it should be necessary to go out, I peeped out, as there was no sound of aircraft. It was a most beautiful night with stars winking between the balloons, which literally looked like a swarm of flies in the sky. We got out our knitting and when I heard planes overhead, I tried to look as though I hadn't heard them. I cannot tell the sound of German planes from English, though I am repeatedly assured by superior male folk that 'it's quite easy to do, as our engines run more sweetly than the German ones.' The idea that any airplane engine that is out to pour death on defenseless people can do anything 'sweetly' does not commend itself to me. I went out at the all clear signal and the dawn was just trembling into being. The sky was a silvery green and in the east there was the faintest flush of pink. It was lovely and the scents from the roses, iris, peonies, etc. so exquisite in the fresh morning air, it was impossible almost to believe that we had been in danger of a horrible death.

The raid, as far as Sheffield was concerned, lasted 40 minutes. In some parts of the country they had it for three hours. Very little damage was done anywhere. They did not reach here at all, though they covered 12 counties.

June 8, 1940

Out of bed again 1:30 a.m. I was roused so suddenly out of a nice sleep that I felt quite sick. Oh, that horrible siren! Yesterday was one of the hottest days of the year and everyone was worn out with the loss of sleep and the heat and now we are up again. I hope it won't be a nightly occurrence.

Much later – The raid only lasted 30 minutes for us. I understand from the early news that they only penetrated eight counties this time. It was terribly hot and it is so difficult to get to sleep again after being up and down stairs, especially after the feeling of helpless fear it gives you. I insist that Doris and I are fully dressed. I believe that being properly dressed has a good psychological effect, even if only unconsciously, and we never know whether we may not have to run out, leave the house altogether, and seek shelter elsewhere. So it is as well to be clothed, if not in one's right mind, at least in one's right clothes!

In case USA is ever at war with a nation that can reach them quickly by air, I would strongly recommend Americans to cultivate the tea habit and learn to make it successfully, for it has a wonderfully soothing effect and most people here make a cup of tea as soon as they get down. After all, you want something to persuade your tummy to stop sinking to uncomfortable depths and accompanied by a biscuit or two, a drink of tea helps to restore your hopes that nothing will happen this time.

Last night they came a quarter of an hour earlier than the night before. If they come a quarter of an hour earlier each night, they will soon be coming before we go to bed, which will be so much more convenient than being waked by ghastly screeching, scrambling into one's clothes in the dark, collecting coats and gas masks, and getting downstairs in five minutes or less.

I am sorry for the men in the big works to be out of bed for some hours, for many of them are on ARP (Air Raid Precaution) duty in addition to their ordinary work and then to have to go to work at furnaces and boilers in this terrific heat. No wonder they are tired!

An aeroplane has just gone overhead. A bomber too. I wondered if it were British and quickly decided if it were not, someone would do something and do it pretty quickly so I went on writing!

The garden is a blaze of colours and nearly all the grass is brown and dried up. There were peals of thunder a little while ago. I would rather a thunder storm came in the night and then we could not have an air raid. We still shouldn't sleep, but we should not have to get up – at least most likely not. Another airplane! I will darn my stockings which have behaved abominably lately in the manner of ladders and holes! and not think of aeroplanes. There's another!

June 9, 1940

Thank goodness we had no air raid warnings during the night. Yesterday the heat was terrible and it was absolutely suffocatingly hot during the night. We went to bed early as we fully expected German visitors during the night. Mercifully they did not come, but I found it impossible to sleep. It is cloudless and baking again today. It seems dreadful to think of men fighting such awful battles in this lovely weather and great heat.

They have discovered that many of the enemy troops in Norway were Austrians who were taken there as tiny children refugees in the last war, brought up by kindly Norwegian folk, given food, homes, etc. Now they are showing their gratitude to their benefactors by devastating their country, the beautiful land of Norway. It seems a specially dirty trick as, of course, these men learned to speak Norwegian as little children and can speak it fluently so they are able to penetrate all over by that means. Is there any dirty, double dealing cruel trick the Nazis cannot evolve? You will also see in the *Sunday Times* an account of Nazi aircraft bombing a lifeboat.

We are wondering what Italy will do. By 'we' I mean ordinary folk with no inside knowledge like myself. My own personal opinion is (for what it is worth) that Mussolini fears that if Hitler sinks he as another dictator will sink also, and he won't want that, so suppose he will come in against us. If so, goodness knows who else will be stirred up against him or against us.

The midday news told us that Nazi aircraft attacked Swiss planes. What on earth do they want to attack an uninterfering neutral like

Switzerland for? Poor little Switzerland – another unoffending little country. Won't Germans be hated the world over for generations and it will serve them right?

Today is a day of national thanksgiving for the evacuation of the BEF (British Expeditionary Force) from Dunkirk. It really does seem to have been divine intervention during those anxious days, for the English Channel is notorious for its weather and rough crossings and yet the sea was smooth enough for rowing boats and even a canoe to cross and recross rescuing our men, placed in such awful plight by ex-King Leopold. A man with a canoe crossed and back three times, each time with one man in it. It was all he had to offer in the way of a boat and he went himself and saved three men's lives. That was a wonderful piece of bravery. Everything that could float nearly was offered to the navy and there were thousands of yachts, fishing cobbles, and rowing boats besides the naval vessels, merchant navy ships, tugs, trawlers, etc. The miracle of such small craft safely plying back and forth from Britain to Dunkirk, over and over again, is comparable with the drying up of the Red Sea to allow the Israelites to pass over when pursued by Pharaoh's armies – and so today Britain is returning thanks for another miracle. I am afraid we so often forget to say 'Thank You', yet we rush to pray for assistance when things go wrong!

There is a good deal that I would like to tell you. I have been considering how to word it and have decided I had perhaps better not say anything. I don't want to write anything I should not.

June 10, 1940

There are humorous situations during air raids. An air raid warden – such a being to be known henceforth as ARW – having carefully parked his wife in their air raid shelter and told her on no account to move out of it till he returned, was making for his post with all possible speed when he met a woman with nine children running up a steep hill looking for an air raid shelter. He took her to his own shelter and his wife calmed her down and he once more went back to his duty. A few hours later he returned home – the ARWs always have to stay at their posts for a given time after the 'all clear' in case the raiders return or in case they are needed in any way – and went to the shelter to release his wife, the woman and her nine children. To his astonishment, there they all were calmly sitting in two rows wearing their gas masks! looking the picture of resignation. 'What on earth have you got those things on for?' he asked. 'Well, we heard the whistles and thought that was the gas signal.' 'How many times have I told you that rattles are the gas signal?' 'Well, I can't remember and I thought we'd be on the safe side!' The ARW said he's never seen anything so funny as when he opened the door and was confronted with all the thirteen gas masks turned inquiringly towards him. 'Thank goodness, I can wipe my nose now. I wanted to and you wouldn't let me before I put my gas mask on.' was the remark of the eldest girl to her mother!

A large number of the BEF, Belgian and French soldiers, came here for a short time after the evacuation. All the small boys are running up to them armed with exercise books asking for their autographs. In future years those books might be quite valuable. Who knows, there might be a signature of some yet-to-be famous man?

The men were brought here in busloads and policemen were detailed to take them to the homes of folk who had arranged to take them in. As one busload came in, two small boys about seven and eight years old respectively, hovered around and finally screwed up their courage to approach an amiable looking officer accompanied by a fierce looking sergeant. The boys asked if their two soldiers had arrived. The fierce sergeant sorted out the two extremely tall soldiers who were to be the boy's parent guests. Said eight years old gravely to seven years old: 'Thee get t'other side and I'll go this side. We'll take care of them, mister. We'll see them quite safe.' and the little group walked off amid the tender smiles of the bystanders which turned to tears as the younger boy looked up at these tired, battle worn men back from the greatest battle in history and said stoutly: 'You'll be quite safe with us.' A world of pride in their little faces as they led the soldiers to their home and their Mum who would surely have everything ready for them and welcome them as only Yorkshire men and women can.

June 11, 1940

So Italy is against us after all. Mussolini hasn't been able to see that if Hitler wins, then Italy will only be allowed what Hitler wishes. If Hitler goes under, then that will be the end of Mussolini too. Count Ciano definitely told Sir Percy Loraine, our ambassador, that the reason why Italy was going to fight us was because France and Britain were rich countries. The old burglar! I should think the four European dictators would be an example to the rest of the world to never, never, never under any circumstances whatever, allow themselves to be governed by a dictator.

We had another peaceful night – inland, at any rate. I was told a perfectly true but very funny story this a.m. In some recent mock air raids for the practice of the wardens, first aiders, fire and ambulance people, they were told in the event of anyone showing panic, the panicky one was to be knocked down and a man volunteered to be a panic casualty. A girl ambulance driver came along, saw the 'panic', jumped out of her ambulance, tore off her tin hat, and brought it down with all her might on the man's head! Result – a real casualty! – a huge lump on the top of the man's head and roars of laughter from everyone except the man himself. The man was lucky to have nothing worse. She might easily have split his skull. Those tin hats are very heavy! The man says: 'Next time they want a volunteer casualty, they can find someone else.' He thinks he's done his bit!

I wonder if you heard Mr. Duff Cooper's (head of the Ministry of Information) speech last p.m. I should have liked to have heard President Roosevelt, but as it was not until 12:15 a.m., I felt I needed sleep more and I knew I should be able to read it in the papers. How thankful you all must be that you do not live in Europe!

> **NOTE:** On 10 June the French government abandoned Paris and fled to southern France. The city was occupied by the German Army and their troops marched down the Champs-Élysées to the Arc de Triomphe on 14 June.

June 14, 1940

I have been trying to write the last chapters of my book, but I cannot concentrate. Poor old France. Paris, lovely Paris, in the hands of those brutal barbarians. It is unthinkable. It was a relief to hear in the 1 o'clock news that the BEF complete with equipment had landed in France. Prime Minister Reynaud has appealed to the USA. I wonder what they will do. You over there know so little of the horrors of warfare, that it is difficult for you to imagine what it is like.

My insomnia has proved extremely useful to the police! Had I been asleep, I could never have observed what I did. I am afraid I had better say no more. I do not want to give anything away that I shouldn't. But the fifth columnists in this country are really a menace and everything is being done to catch them. I cannot conceive the kind of mind that will live in a decent country, enjoy all its freedoms and privileges, and then try to give away information that would cause damage or ruin lives and property. A working woman said the other day that she didn't remember seeing the country so lovely before and added: 'Doesn't all this make you love England more?' There are national beauty spots all around this city and we don't want them spoiled. But neither do we want enemy planes guided here by the action of fifth columnists.

How I wish I felt free to say all I would like. There is no official censorship of letters, but you never know into whose hands they might fall other than yours, and if other eyes should read them unsympathetically and use anything I have said so that they should harm my dear old England, I should never forgive myself.

It is a week tonight since Sheffield had its last air raid warning. I wish I thought it would be the last! I have a hopeful nature, but not as hopeful as that. I find that maple sugar is not rationed and thought I would supplement my allowance, but found the price was too prohibitive. It has gone up a lot. So has honey, which I love. A friend once gave me some honey she had sent from Florida – orange blossom honey. It was good.

Yesterday I watched a lot of balloons going up. One burst when up in the sky and an old lady of nearly 80 at whose house I'd gone for tea said: 'Oh! Is it a parachutist? Are you sure it isn't a parachutist?' Her son and I had quite a job to reassure her. It looked most peculiar flapping about while they hauled it down. My comment was: 'Bang! There goes 200 pounds.' But I personally should find the price of one balloon only, a perfect godsend! Isn't war wasteful?

June 16, 1940

This morning I went with a friend to the fire station to learn how to deal with incendiary bombs, the fires they cause, and the people who collapse by being overcome by smoke. I should think there were about 80 to 100 householders like myself who had gone for instruction – both men and women. We all roared with laughing when the fireman instructor was demonstrating with another fireman how to remove any collapsed person from a burning room. He told us that a few weeks ago he saw someone drag a person from a room by the feet and set off downstairs as fast as they could, with the woman's head banging on each stair as they went. By the time they had reached the bottom, the woman had recovered her senses – and the use of her tongue!!!

Later, along with a few others – of whom I was the eldest – I donned a fireman's overall and crawled along on hands and knees into a room filled with nauseating green smoke as a 'test'. We went three at a time and as the other two were men, the fireman was inclined to be a bit lenient to 'the lady,' but I told him I had come to learn, so moved up close to the fire. We all lay flat on the (very dirty) floor. They shut the door on us and smoked us as long as they thought we could stand it. I was surprised to find that crawling along, head nearly touching the floor, we were able to breathe without choking. Standing up, we should have been suffocated in no time. I wanted to laugh – we must have looked bonny objects from behind. I was the first one to enter but when we turned around to come out, I heard one of the men say he had lost his sense of direction. Of course we couldn't see anything but smoke and the floor – and the fireman made him feel his way around by the wall like we had been told to do by the instructor. He told me to lead the way out, so I could not see what the others looked like. But those watching us go into the burning hut said they wished they'd had cameras – we looked like we were just going to enjoy a game of bears. Then they exploded a bomb and gave a practical demonstration of all the instruction we had heard. I wielded the hose, as we had been told to do on the floor, walls, and roof first, then the fire, and lastly the bomb which only had to be sprayed gently. I quite enjoyed manipulating the switch on the nozzle which regulated the jet or spray of water, whichever you wanted. In fact, I enjoyed it so much I nearly drenched a perspiring fireman who was working the pump! But it really brought all the horrors of air raids very near. Especially when we were told that one plane could carry 1,000 to 1,500 bombs and when we saw all the damage one incendiary bomb could do!

The drought still continues and the moors outside the city have been badly burnt, some think by fifth columnists. Whether as a signal to enemy aircraft or any other signal ordinary folk like us do not know. Of course it may only have been careless hikers. They have been fired before by careless folk. I am very sickened by the smell of burning moors. I live so close to them and how I love them. I believe you have nothing to correspond to them in the US. You don't know what heather looks like, do you? Heather honey is delicious I think, but some people don't care for the flavour. A great deal of the stuff sold as honey over here, I am sure has never seen a bee and yet in the 16th century and centuries before that, every householder in England kept their own bees. Bee keeping is intensely interesting and fascinating. It is one of the many things I want to do some day in the future, if possible, when we are at peace again. There is a very old superstition that bees know when war is coming. I wrote an article once on bee superstitions.

NOTE: *On 18 June, Winston Churchill broadcast this famous speech over the radio:*

What General Weygand called the Battle of France is over. I expect that the Battle of Britain is about to begin. Upon this battle depends the survival of Christian civilisation. Upon it depends our own British life, and the long continuity of our institutions and our Empire. The whole fury and might of the enemy must very soon be turned on us. Hitler knows that he will have to break us in this Island or lose the war. If we can stand up to him, all Europe may be free and the life of the world may move forward into broad, sunlit uplands. But if we fail, then the whole world, including the United States, including all that we have known and cared for, will sink into the abyss of a new Dark Age made more sinister, and perhaps more protracted, by the lights of perverted science. Let us therefore brace ourselves to our duties, and so bear ourselves that, if the British Empire and its Commonwealth last for a thousand years, men will still say, 'This was their finest hour'.

June 19, 1940

I thought I had better try and send a line, if possible, before we are in the thick of it over here after the way France has given in. Of course, now we do not know what evil methods the Germans will adopt toward us. It is not for me to express an opinion over France's attitude, but it makes me personally feel that we ought never to trust any other country again. All the same, I cannot think that a great nation like the French will let itself be governed by an old man of eighty-five and go back on all they swore and pledged to do. Thank goodness we got rid of all our ancient generals etc. at the beginning of the war.

England has its back to the wall and we feel now that they have brought back large numbers of men from France, that we are all shut in together and we have each other 'in this snug little, tight little island' of ours (as the old music hall song of ours goes) and together we'll face what comes.

Being a woman of no importance in the world, I cannot expect America to take any notice of me, but my strong advice to that great country is PREPARE. Hitler is after America too, so make no mistake about that. He may be at you next. World domination is his self-admitted goal. He will have to do something, for he ruins and destroys wherever he goes. They have eaten all the hogs they got from Denmark, Holland's farmlands were flooded, Belgium's destroyed, Russia's wheat crop has been bad, French farmlands devastated, our empire will not supply him or Italy. America is his only hope. He knows you have no army worth his consideration – so he thinks – your navy he thinks could not keep him out. His air force – in his opinion – can conquer the world. When it meets the RAF (Royal Air Force) planes, it frequently turns and flies away on the principle that 'he who turns and runs away lives to fight another day.' Saving themselves for attacking England, I suppose.

Lovely little England. Last night about 11:30 there was a full moon and I went out in the garden to smell all the sweet scents before going to bed. How peaceful and pretty it looked. Will it look like that at 11:30 tonight? I wonder? Even at that very moment, evil things were flying about not so very far away, though I did not know it then.

I wonder if you heard Mr. Churchill's speech on our 8 p.m. news. It was being broadcast to the USA. I think it was about 3 p.m. with you, wasn't it? Well, we are prepared for the Germans and for terrible slaughter amongst ourselves. I for one most certainly do not want to die. Why should one man in the world have the power to cause suffering, ruin and death to millions who have never harmed him or his country? They have, of course, evacuated thousands of children. No doubt it will be the aim of the Germans to visit those places especially and bomb every child they can. That is the kind of thing they do. They pride themselves on that kind of behaviour. All our men are ready to receive the parachutists. Some of them are quite looking forward to greeting them!!!

I enclose a funny cartoon, for we laugh. Oh yes, we laugh. If we didn't, we could not carry on. In fact, I've been getting a good teasing because I have a walking stick that was my father's and you pull out the handle and lo, a beautiful sharp sword in perfect condition. I happened to say I must take it out and have it by me in the next air raid. They have been telling me that I must run and spike the bomb on the end of the sword and then proceed to put my fire training into practice! I meant to use it if I thought I'd meet a parachutist. Friends seem to think they had better give me a wide berth in case of mistaken identity. For once spiked, they might be no more use to England. They don't seem to have much faith in my judgement, and less in my aim. One never is appreciated properly in one's own town!!

I hope our ships will come in your convoys as suggested. Then communication with the USA should be a bit easier. There is such a lot of gardening to do, but I haven't the heart to do it what with the winter damage, summer drought, and now the everlasting uncertainty of life. We still have plenty of food, please let that be known all over. In spite of the drought my little front garden attracts a good deal of attention from passersby. One lot of friends are very disgusted with me that I didn't dig it all up and plant vegetables. In vain I protested that the soil would need a great deal of money I don't possess to be spent on it before it could begin to produce anything edible and it would not be really satisfactory for nearly two years, by which time (and before) I am hoping to be in the USA if there is any opening for me. Though of course I did not tell them that. As they are not gardeners, they think because I can grow shrubs and flowers, vegetables will flourish like the Psalmist's green bay tree. I get so cross with people who do not know anything about it when they tell me my 'duty.'

There were about 100 planes off the east coast last night. Most of them flew away when our terrific anti-aircraft barrage began to play the band. Our people brought down seven of the remaining ones and damaged some more. I should think it is highly probable we shall be attacked every night now while this moon lasts. The balloons are going up all over the place at this very moment, so I may have to seize my belongings and fly. Oh dear, I do hope not – it's so lovely in the garden.

June 21, 1940

I was just drowsy when Wailing Willie, seeming more insistent than ever, wailed us all out of bed at 12:10 a.m. With us the air raid lasted four hours, in some places five hours. We could hear bombs dropping in the distance now and again but, mercifully, we escaped. The news told us that there had been more than a hundred planes over England. It was wonderful to find how very little damage they inflicted considering the number.

The a.m. we all received a printed pamphlet 'What To Do In An Invasion.' Most of it seems common sense, which people ought to exercise without pamphlets being given to them. But I suppose it is largely a matter of keeping cool and resourceful. I hope I may keep my head if I am called upon to do so.

June 26, 1940

Well, aren't things in a bonny mess? I personally feel that now we have not to carry the responsibility of the French as well as ourselves, we can do what we like without consulting anyone else. If the French colonies refuse to surrender to the twin robbers, then Hitler will be in a quandary. They'll have to send armies to quell them and with no navy, how will he send them?

We were called up for three hours night before last and last night one and a quarter hours. And the annoying thing was we had only been back in bed for twenty-five minutes when Willie wailed again. I wish I could do something violent to somebody!! We had only been downstairs for five minutes when Shouting Sam told us all clear. Rumor hath it that the second warning was a mistake and that one of our affectionately named balloons got loose. Someone saw it cavorting about the city. Its cables caught on a chimney pot and the householders thought they were being bombed. Agitated specials were convinced it was a Heinkel bomber and so we're all fetched out of bed. I'm afraid it would be indiscreet to mention the name of the balloon as she is held in great affection for a reason I've never been able to fathom. Maybe it is all a tale, though quite true a balloon did break loose.

It seems a nightly performance now to hear Wailing Willie and looks like being more so till the war ends and the Tiger and the Jackal – so aptly named by one of your US Senators! – have had their fangs drawn. But to be fetched down after twenty-five minutes and return to bed just for ten minutes was more rousing than being up all the time. Sleep seemed extra difficult to attain and I could not get warm. I've been cold all day. I was obliged to go into the city this a.m. Everyone joked about the splendid night they'd had and most people looked very weary. I am arranging that Doris and I take it turn and turn about to go to bed at 7 p.m. in order to get some rest. I have no obligation to a scoundrel like Hitler turning me into a nervous wreck for lack of sleep. Most people are planning out their rest periods so Hitler can carry on. So shall we in our own way.

During the air raids I usually knit. I have nearly finished a Shetland wool scarf of four colours that I have done during my nightly uprisings. It would not have been nearly so quickly finished if it had not been for Hitler. That is something I must thank him for.

Thank goodness I went to boarding school and there learned to dress quickly. I have always been able to dress in five minutes – washing included! I have long hair too! It usually seems to go up much more effectively in an air raid when I'm doing it in the dark, than it ever does when I'm dressing for a lecture or to speak at a dinner on which occasions I brush it well and take endless pains over it! But to dress in five minutes in the dark with Wailing Willie sending cold shivers down your spine is no easy matter. I expect to reduce my handicap and do it in less. One night I did it in less than two – collected gas mask and coat and was downstairs before Willie's final groans died away, but I had not done my hair. If you do not already know from experience, you have no idea how perverse ordinary garments could be in such circumstances. They show a marked preference to go on back to front, to elude one's grasp, and to tear in inconvenient places, given to stick and refuse to slip into their appointed positions. Coat hangers decline to leave coats; belts prefer the floor to one's waist.

June 28, 1940

We have had two full nights in bed. I cannot hope we shall get a third. By some lucky means, we escaped the attention of Hitler's minions.

I have just been watching an army service lorry containing soldiers. The lorry has a big 'L' back and front to indicate learner. The men changed places just outside the house and the man now trying to drive is alternately starting with a terrific jerk, going a few yards and then stopping dead. The men in the lorry are all offering him advice at once and he looks very flurried and cross! It was really funny to see him though he himself did not seem to find anything amusing in the situation. While he was at a standstill and unable to start again, one of the soldiers called out to him: 'Mind you sound your horn. It's not safe going at this rate!'

June 30, 1940

We have had three nights in our beds. That does not mean enemy planes did not come to England, but that it was not considered necessary to call us up. I must not tell you where the damage was as our Powers That Be do not tell us the names of the places as that would tell the Germans where they were. But they tell us how many killed and wounded, how many planes we bring down, and how many we lose. Sometimes they tell us how many planes come over. In last night's raid on this country an infirmary (hospital) was hit.

I now have another adoption in the Navy. I think I told you a boy with a very good education wanted to go in the Navy and the only way he could manage it was to enlist as a stoker. He wrote me a most cheerful letter which I received yesterday and said in it: 'To think I spent years rotting on an office stool, when I might have been in the Navy.' He is expecting to join the Ajax eventually and thinks life in the Navy – even as a stoker – is perfect. The beauty of it is he is terribly seasick every time he goes to sea! He regards that as a tiresome joke.

I am letting a few of my plants go to seed – a thing I would never allow ordinarily – and am going to send them to Barbara for her garden. I shall love to see some of my own garden in yours when I come to the land of Peace and Hurry. They will also be a form of bribery to get an extra letter!

NOTE: *Barbara was Charles and Jane Beaumont's 12-year-old daughter.*

July 2, 1940

Tomorrow I am going to a small town near here to try to persuade the owners of some large nurseries to grow medicinal plants. I have had strong appeals from drug importers and the Association of British Chemical Manufacturers to see if I can get anything going that will produce more drugs. As the appeals have been sent through the suggestion of the Ministry of Health, I am hoping to get something done somewhere. I wrote two letters to the Sheffield newspapers making an appeal and offering to give all necessary information to any enquirers. I am wondering if anyone will take the trouble to enquire. Everyone is mad on growing food and I have pointed out that the response to 'Dig For Victory' was wonderful, but that 'Dig For Healing' was equally necessary. But people are awfully wooden over such things.

By the way, if you hear on the wireless any time: 'This is the New British Broadcasting Station', beware for it is anything but British. It is German and is used to propagate their lying tales. Please let everyone know this. I was much surprised to hear Raymond Gram Swing on the air again, for we were told that he had to give up broadcasting. I hope I may meet him someday, but perhaps he will be too grand for me to meet.

I do hope we shall have a peaceful night as I want to appear at my best when interviewing a canny businessman about drug growing and not feeling like a piece of chewed string with my brains like boiled mashed turnips and looking like a faded octogenarian who has spent the night in the tool shed! It is doubly necessary to be alert when you are out to persuade a man to do something he has no intention of doing, isn't it? I should like to tell you about the air raids, but you never know who might see the paper and the Germans might then get to know where exactly they have been. Up to the time of writing, we are all right here. The damage that has been done is relatively slight everywhere, but we fully expect much worse to come.

July 3, 1940

I duly got me to Chesterfield to interview the proprietor of some very large nurseries. The interview was much more successful than I had dared to hope. When I got home I found that a reporter from our evening paper had been up to see me. I wrote two letters to our local newspapers and one of them – to quote their own words – 'thought it too good to be left as a letter' and interviewed me over the phone in a great hurry so that they could get their article in before the morning papers stole their thunder!!

I heard the postman and raced downstairs in the hope of word from someone in the US but they are having nothing to do with me seemingly! I must possess my soul in patience. I keep forgetting to say that if you know any American volunteers who are coming over here to serve in our forces, do let me know and let them have my address too. So long as they are nice, I don't mind how humble their rank. I should be glad to see them. Two American airmen broadcast tonight. They came over to volunteer and one (if not both) is in the Royal Air Force.

It is a most wonderful evening, nine o'clock and bright clear sky. I do not see how we can get through the night in peace. But oh! I hope so.

July 4, 1940

After a peaceful night my birthday and a house full of lovely flowers. To cheer me still further four replies by afternoon post in response to my appeal. Am beginning to feel I've set myself a huge job. That is what I really like, but in this case so much depends on so many other things. I am now going to tackle 1) government 2) Ministry of Health 3) Horticulture Trades Association 4) British Pharmaceutical Society 5) British manufacturing chemists 6) my member of Parliament and any number of lesser fry who can be persuaded (or goaded) into toeing the line! Each one of them ought to be approached first. How am I to do it?

NOTE: *10 July 1940 was the start of the Battle of Britain.*

July 11, 1940

Another nice letter from you not opened by the censor and a copy of *Life* magazine. I am looking forward to reading that. I foolishly accepted an invitation out to tea today and am swamped with work to do with the drug growing, but I feel extremely woolly and feel that a change would be wise. I've written about fifty letters the last few days and think my pen would sign my name by itself!

July 12, 1940

I'm quite looking forward to American food, the descriptions of it in the US books always make me hungry! I'm practicing now to do with less tea, as we are only allowed two ounces per head for our ration. I feel I've not had a proper breakfast unless I've had coffee, so hope that won't be rationed too.

The thought of your 'cottage by the lake' brings back the happy days of childhood when I spent three or four months of every year (up to my 27th year, in fact) in the West Highlands of Scotland. The most beautiful part of Britain.

The fiat has gone forth now that no air raid sirens will be sounded till they are actually upon us, as the warnings meant such a lot of lost time to the armament works. Steel had to be left to cool and then it took three days to bring it back to normal output. It is not giving civilians much chance to seek safety, but we have to risk it in the interests of the safety of the services and the country. It will be a fearful scramble to get one's things and be downstairs in half a minute. We shall have to dress downstairs having left something we most needed in our rooms, or dropped them somewhere enroute! I foresee some funny styles of dress in future night raids. Daylight air raids won't be at all funny. Before, we had five minutes to seek shelter – now we shall have half a minute if that. Everyone in the country is wishing that Hitler would begin his promised invasion. Wouldn't it be a sell if he never tried, on account of trouble in France and the Balkans? I think the little bounder is beginning to feel he has bitten off more than he can chew already and Italy up to the present time has been no help at all to him.

I expect Americans – some of them anyway – know a lot more about some of our famous places than many inhabitants of these islands do. I was well over thirty before I had seen the Ruskin Museum in Sheffield and then it was only because a devotee of Ruskin from the south was in Sheffield and wanted to see it, so I took her! Yet I know more about Edinburgh and York than many of the folk who live in those ancient cities do!

I much enjoyed *Life* magazine and have lent it round and am going to send it to J.M. when we have all finished it. J.M. and all the ship's company love the US papers you send. I wonder if the photo of me in my gas mask has arrived? I hope you don't show that to anyone in order to impress them with my appearance!

Later – A glorious thunderstorm is raging and although it is only about 6:15 p.m., I have my reading lamp on. The rain is terrific. We cannot have an air raid in a storm like this and that is a great cause for gratitude. I said once that I couldn't tell the difference between an English and a German plane. I no longer am so ignorant.

Be sure never to take any notice of the New British Broadcasting Station. It is GERMAN, not British at all and be careful of French broadcasts – they too are German.

I am prepared to like America and love Americans. Everyone that has been to the US is full of their kindness to strangers. And after all, kindness means such a lot. I'm looking forward to my visit tremendously.

NOTE: *On 19 July Hitler delivered a speech to the Reichstag in Berlin which was what he called an 'appeal to reason' to avert 'destruction of a great world empire', but he made it clear that rejection would mean an attack with all of the forces at the command of the Axis powers. 'I do this not as a victor, but for the triumph of common sense.' Without delivering any ultimatum, Hitler said that it had never been his desire to destroy the British Empire. He warned against interpreting his appeal as weakness and said that 'Churchill may parry my words with the claim that I feel doubt or fear, but in any case I will have my knowledge that I acted rightly, according to my conscience'. He then said that his cardinal aims in foreign policy had been friendship with Britain and with Italy. 'Despite my sincere efforts it has not been possible,' he said, 'to achieve the friendship with England which I believed would have been blessed by both. What is coming will visit the people, not Churchill, who will probably be in Canada.' Hitler said that in caustic reference to the British prime minster as a warning to the British people of the effects of a blitzkrieg attack.*

July 21, 1940

I expect many Americans are anxious about us over here. Don't be. We still have plenty to eat. Our air force is a magnificent one. We don't pretend that there are no air raids on these islands, there are, bombs are dropped, but our determination to stand up to the bullies at all costs is as great as ever.

Hitler's speech showed the world that he would gladly get out of coming to grips with us if he could. Things have not gone quite the way he wished, although he has now got France. It will be a liability for he will have to feed it and as he can't feed his own Germans, he will have to work miracles – which he can't do.

The spirit here is universal. We have now got only ourselves to please, no other armies or navies to consult. Mr. Churchill always gets what he sets out to get and the country is solidly behind him.

We now have to carry our identification cards with the added information as to our next of kin in case of death or injury through air raids; our gas masks, of course, we are not to travel in certain areas and if challenged, are always to stop and produce evidence of who we are and, if necessary, why we are in that particular place. I personally have not yet been asked for any information, though when business took me into a certain government building the other day, soldiers were on guard with fixed bayonets at all kinds of unexpected places and corners. They looked so absolutely motionless and statue-like, that I should dearly have loved to tweak one of them under the rifle arm just to see what would happen. But I have so often been told by serious folk when I have wanted to do or say something startling, that 'we are at war'. Plus I thought the consequences might hinder me from getting on with any effort to produce enough drugs for our manufacturing chemists! Indeed, I might have needed drugs myself. Those bayonets looked so very sharp and efficient – real 'Sheffield blades' as the saying is. In these days any suspects are firmly and promptly dealt with without any preliminary polite parley.

I feel very sad when I think of some of our beautiful old houses and public buildings many hundreds of years old with all their treasures possibly being bombed to bits.

Our navy is of course wonderful. I wonder what the spirit of Sir Francis Drake is thinking as he looks down on Plymouth Avenue – or he did before the war. I don't know whether they have removed his statue for safety. If so, I'm sure he won't like it for all British schoolboys know that when the Spanish Armada was sighted beating up the channel, he was playing a game of bowls. When they told Sir Francis these big ships were coming, he replied: 'When I have finished, I will attend to the Spanish ships.' – and he did!

Sir Francis Drake's drum hangs over the entrance to the home of his descendants and whenever England is in danger, invisible hands beat the drum. The roll of that drum was heard in 1914 and it was heard again in 1939. But the spirit of Sir Francis Drake is to be found in thousands of our young heroes today and the drum did not beat in vain, for they poured into recruiting offices, naval stations and anywhere where they could help. Everything that the country is asked to do, it does promptly and if it is something inconvenient, then it is made a joke and there is one more score against Hitler when the day of reckoning comes. For the first time in our island history, we are subjected to all kinds of restrictions, rules and regulations, but nobody minds a tinker's cuss and the comedians bring down the music halls with roars of laughter over them.

I think I told you about my father's sword stick in my last letter. I'm quite grieved because nobody seems to have much faith in my successful aim if a parachutist appears in my garden! In fact, after dark the other night I thought I heard someone about and went to look – very cautiously – and forgot all about the sword stick till I discovered that there was no one there at all. In spite of what people say, I find the sword stick a great source of courage – especially when there is no danger!

It is good of you to say come now, but I believe we are only allowed to take ten pounds out of the country with us. I believe that is $40 and that would not take me very far, so I must have some literary work over there to eke out until such time as lecture seasons begin. I am looking forward to coming and expecting to enjoy every minute of it. There are lots of things I want to see and do quite apart from my work – Niagara, Yosemite Valley, your lake, travel in a pullman, see all sorts of people and so on. I am reading *America Expects* by Hector Bolitho, who went for a lecture tour in USA. It rather frightened me. I don't think I could rise to such dizzy heights as he did.

I broke off just then to hear a broadcast from South Africa by General Smuts. I don't think Hitler would like his speech very much! He said if the Germans could not beat us or stop the evacuation at Dunkirk in a single concentrated stop, then it was extremely unlikely that with many miles of ocean, sky, and land for them to attack and defend, that they would not conquer us at all. The transmission was very bad, but he painted a terrible but true picture of Europe and the world if the Germans did win. I think it is a pity that some US pro-Germans don't have to live in a country under German protection. They would soon want to buzz back to America, freedom, and plenty.

I am sending off the *Life* magazine and two picture papers to J.M. I haven't heard for nearly a fortnight. I do hope he's all right. The navy has been having a strenuous time lately. He said in his last letter he was afraid they would find it very dull in peace times. I can see Sir Francis Drake smile. I saw a picture of his ghost once; he looks like a very nice man. I think I should have enjoyed talking to him – him I mean, not his spook. I wish men dressed nowadays as they did then. They would look so much more attractive and I cannot see that the most becoming ruffs would be any more uncomfortable than the modern, starched turndown collars. Though admittedly they would take a lot of time to get up. Do you use that expression? A service gas mask and a ruff do not seem to combine very well, though, but no doubt sailors would get over a little difficulty of the kind.

Some friends of mine in Halifax have got two evacuees from Guernsey (Channel Islands), a mother and a mentally deficient daughter. The poor woman was some time before she could get to know where her other children had been sent and even now is uncertain as to the whereabouts of her husband. She thinks he may have been left in Germany. The Germans have occupied the islands. They will be very little use to them you may be sure, or we should not have evacuated them.

A girl was telling me a story of some brave girls in the ATS (Auxiliary Territorial Service – the women's branch of the British army.) Her brother told her and as he took part in the episode, it is firsthand and true. There were some girls in the ATS in Paris, telephone girls connected with our forces. Everyone was making for Dunkirk, when the colonel suddenly remembered them and asked for volunteers to go back to Paris to fetch them. The girl's brother was one of the volunteers. He felt a bit annoyed at having to waste valuable time over two or three girls – so he says! When they got to Paris, bombs were raining down on the city, but there were these three girls still at their telephones. The men had some difficulty in persuading them that they must leave, as the Germans were then entering the city. The whole way back to the coast was a nightmare of bombing and whenever German raiders saw the car with British soldiers and three girls in it, they made a special point of attacking it with machine guns. He says the girls never let out a squeal or showed funk at all. They turned a bit green, but that was all and jumped out and lay in ditches as quickly as seasoned soldiers, made no fuss and tried not to be a trouble to the men who had rescued them. He says all the men were tremendously impressed with their behaviour and that he personally will never think of girls as being squealing cowards in any circumstances. He said it was hats off to those three girls all the time. I should like to be able to record that romantic attachments resulted from the experience but once in safety, they never saw each other afterwards!

July 27, 1940

I could not come to America by the boats bringing children as you suggested, as no one is to be allowed to stay and only a suitcase in the way of luggage is permitted. I shall be obliged to bring my lantern slides, typewriter, a certain number of reference books besides my clothes – which wouldn't cram into a suitcase!

I explained in my last letter that we are only allowed to bring ten pounds (I think $40) out of the country. That would not pay my expenses for long in New York while interviewing agents etc. It would not go far in railway fares I imagine and I most certainly cannot sit down and vegetate on kind relatives. I want to see them all, every one of them, but not to be a burden to any of them. So if I can procure a few commissioned articles, I might manage until the lecture season begins, unless of course I am lucky enough to start off with a few lectures. I expect to enjoy everything in America – except the tea! and that is nothing! I am to give my lantern lecture, the Folklore of Trees, on August 29th. The idea of a lantern lecture in August is rather unusual, but no one is having seaside holidays this year, so I suppose the sponsors feel that it will be all right. I hope so indeed! I am not used to empty halls.

We are still very much alive and England, Scotland, and Wales are still intact in spite of air raids in various parts of the country. Our broadcasting goes on uninterruptedly. In fact, we had a most thrilling running commentary by a BBC observer on an air battle actually taking place. I am literally bouncing up and down in my chair with excitement. We could hear guns and bombs quite plainly and the commentator sounded as worked up as if he were describing a national football match! We could hear the anti-aircraft men shouting: 'Got it! It's coming down! It's down, it's down!' It was thrilling.

We still have plenty of food, so don't believe it when you hear otherwise on the German wireless. Everyone is regarding as a joke the possibility of parachutists descending in their gardens. In fact, airmen from German bombers and fighters that are disintegrating owing to the attentions of our airmen, frequently come down by parachutes in the queerest places. They are usually dazed or injured, broken legs, etc. and wounded. They do not put up much of a fight, so they are easily dealt with. They are all so surprised that they are not instantly killed or tortured as they have been told in Germany how the British ill treat their prisoners – a piece of lying propaganda that can never be substantiated.

The Germans will defeat their own ends if they sink many more neutral ships as they did the ships bearing the repatriated French. The men who landed in England after being rescued from the sinking ship are so furious that they are joining up under Gen. de Gaulle.

I had occasion to enter into another part of Yorkshire a few days ago. I do not see how any mechanized enemy army could get very far in this country, even if they could land in sufficient numbers. No one is being worried about sea transit, but of course they can do great damage by air raids. I think the two European bullies are surprised at our air efficiency. Mussolini hasn't gained much yet. Hitler will find him a tremendous liability and I do not think that thinking, level-headed Italians were too keen on this war and they won't like it if Hitler has to come to their aid after all Mussolini's boastings about having us trapped in the Mediterranean etc. I think Hitler is trying to start a conflagration in eastern Europe so that we shall have to send men out of England to protect our African possessions as well as Egypt. When we have left England defenseless, then he will step in. Aha Hitler! John Bull is not as easily caught napping and Mr. Churchill does not nap at all where England is concerned.

August 4, 1940

I am going to do all my windows over with a patent kind of varnish which diminishes glass splintering in air raids. There have been almost more injuries from flying glass than from bombs. It flies for hundreds of yards. It is perfectly horrible to look through windows that have been 'treated' but I should look still more horrible if I were injured in the face. The windows make you feel bilious. Some people have plastered them with gummed paper. It makes me dizzy. I've steadily refused to do it, but now feel it might be wiser to do something. The glass breaks just the same but doesn't fly so far.

I am looking forward to seeing you all and have begun making arrangements for the disposal of my specially precious plants in my absence. One or two experienced gardeners have promised to take them and look after them. I wonder when I shall really arrive. Meantime, I look forward to it and get quite excited and thrilled at the thought of it.

August 6, 1940

You will probably have heard that the Germans dropped leaflets over this country last week – copies of Hitler's speech of all things! Some of them fell in a field near a house in which lived an elderly woman. She went out and picked up all she could – sold them as souvenirs in aid of the Red Cross.

I went down into the city this afternoon to the pictures – or as you would say 'the movies'. It was England's most famous comedian in a famous play, *Charlie's Aunt*, which is one long laugh from beginning to end. The picture – or movie – was altered from the play, but was a perfect scream. I simply ached with laughing. We also saw the air battle over Dover harbour (which was broadcast some days ago.) It was very thrilling to watch – in safety. I much prefer the theater any time to the movie or pictures however.

We are still waiting Hitler's blitzkrieg. If it comes, the country is ready. Everybody has the utmost confidence in our navy, air force, and army. The RAF has been truly marvelous.

The shoulder strap on my gas mask case broke today and I all but lost the whole thing. If we lose them, we have to pay for new ones ourselves.

I have often wondered what we shall do with them all after the war is over. In the pictures this afternoon they showed us a gas drill onboard a HM battleship. J.M. says their gas masks are far more comfortable to wear than ours. I wish I could buy a service mask. The men will need to be as comfortable as possible and not hampered in any way with submarines and aircraft to attend to. Both ends at once, so to speak!

August 9, 1940

Do you remember me telling about a sailor who was brought up in a very nice home and who was determined to get into the navy somehow? The only possible way was to enlist as a stoker. Never shall I forget his father's horror. It does seem rather a waste of brains, but he is certain to get promotion very quickly. He writes me the most delightful letters. As we know a great many of the same people, we can share some good jokes. Well, yesterday afternoon I attended his wedding, he had gotten seven days leave. The invitation came less than 24 hours previously. Fortunately, I had no engagements so was delighted to go. He is well over six feet with such an awfully nice face and the kind of smile that would get him all sorts of favors less fortunate folk could not buy.

I am feeling very anxious about J.M. The navy has had a grueling time lately and up till now I've not had my usual weekly letter. His sister is to be married a week tomorrow and he cannot get leave for it with things as they are at present. I am looking forward to him staying here whenever he does get leave. I think he will deserve a bit of spoiling and I shall love the doing thereof.

I polished up my sword stick the other a.m. There has been so much joking and teasing about it, that I begin to wonder whether I might not have to use it after all. I should say I would never dare to stick it into anyone, even a parachutist, and a friend said quite emphatically: 'What? You'd never dare? If he landed on one of your precious plants and broke it down, you'd be after him. "Look what you've done to my so and so and stab him fiercely." Ah well, I do not claim to be brave. I only hope I can keep my head and my wits about me when and if the occasion arises.

August 10, 1940

Do you remember me telling you in a recent letter about Drake's drum? The other night a man was broadcasting about the war and mentioned Drake's drum. He told us that it sounded on the eve of the Dunkirk evacuation. The drum is at Buckland Abbey, the ancestral home of the Drake family. Sir Francis Drake himself lived there and the drum, I believe, hangs over the entrance to the abbey. The broadcaster said that endless investigations have been made and it has been established beyond all doubt that no human agency is responsible for its drumming at times of national danger – out of which we shall come successfully.

> **NOTE:** 13 August 1940 was called Adlertag (Eagle Day) by the Germans. In a huge air offensive, the Luftwaffe carried out 1,485 sorties over England and the English Channel. The Germans lost forty-five planes and the British thirteen.

August 13, 1940

Everyone is terribly anxious just at present about their navy and air force friends and relations, with the terrific battle raging. That does not mean that we are gloomy or fearful of defeat. Not at all. Defeat simply does not enter into our heads, but naturally we cannot help thinking of those who are bearing the attack and the fighting themselves. I am quite anxious about J.M. not having heard from him for a fortnight. Of course, I do not know where his ship is, but all our ships seem to annoy the Germans and though they are doing their best to starve us, we are very far from starving. So let that be known please. I think Mr. Hoover is making a mistake. The war will be over a lot quicker if the unfortunate folk whom Hitler is 'protecting' are short of food, for then they will rise up in fury and soon end his tyranny. Even an American statesman ought to know that no matter what Hitler promises, he never keeps his word. So any food sent will most certainly find its way, and quickly too, into the stomachs of the Nazis and the Nazis only. Hitler says they have ample food.

> **NOTE:** 15 August was called The Greatest Day of the Battle of Britain, with the heaviest fighting so far. The Luftwaffe flew over 2,000 sorties and lost seventy-five aircraft. British Fighter Command flew 974 sorties and lost thirty-four aircraft. The day was called 'Black Thursday' in Germany.

August 16, 1940

Well Hitler, what about it now? You were to have been in England and peace was to have been signed in London yesterday. Instead, a thousand of your planes attacked the south and east coasts up to the north of England. You lost 169 planes, we lost 27, but as ten pilots were saved, that counts as 17, as we can replace our machines more easily than pilots.

The Germans dropped more leaflets, which have quickly been named 'bomblets' and also they dropped parachutes to scare the population. Instead of scaring us, however, they and the bomblets have been collected and by the permission of the Lord Lieutenant of the county and the chief of police, they are being auctioned at high prices to raise money for the Red Cross fund.

Nearly 12 months of war and still alive. We did not know months ago whether we should be or not. We do not owe it to the humanity of the Germans but to the skill and daring of our navy and air force. They really are beyond praise. Bless them, they are magnificent!

Yesterday when a German plane was shot down into the sea, a small boat went out to rescue the crew and one of our ordinary seamen went overboard to try to free the wounded German from the wrecked plane, when some enemy planes appeared and machine gunned the crew of the rescue ship and the sailor swimming in the water trying to save the German pilot. There was nothing for it but to haul in the seaman and row back to land, leaving the enemy to sink. The rescue boat was of course only a small rowing boat and the men were quite unarmed – or the dirty skunks would not have attacked it.

A girl went out in a canoe and rescued a sergeant gunner from a wrecked British plane. A boat manned by two men also went and the sergeant said he ducked and kept out of their sight when he saw the girl coming! The men in the other boat rescued the others, thought the sergeant was drowned and made for home. As soon as they'd gone, he bobbed up and floated about waiting for the girl with her canoe. She got him back to shore safely and before the other boat with the men in it arrived! Great enthusiasm for the girl and tremendous amusement over the sergeant.

August 17, 1940

England is feeling very cheerful today. The glorious summer weather which has suddenly returned helps us to feel more cheery still. The large number of planes down are most encouraging. Surely Hitler will begin to realize that we mean business and are not going to give in at his ordering.

I keep hearing gunfire or bombs, but as we are only about 60 miles from the coast as the crow flies and as the wind is in the east, I do not expect to seek shelter hurriedly. The wind carries the sounds very plainly and probably air battles are raging all along the coast. We shall hear about it at 9 p.m. news time. Till then, business as usual.

August 18, 1940

I wish you good people in America would not talk and think of us as a 'beleaguered island.' We are NOT beleaguered! Our ships sail the world over, most of them returned safely to our ports. Our aircraft fly a goodly portion of the globe and also return. To be beleaguered, you've got to be fastened in, unable to get out. We are very much able to get out, as the Germans know to their cost.

I have begun collecting what I shall sell and what I shall store when I come to the US. It makes the visit feel nearer. Mr. C. is going to take charge of most of my precious plants for me in his nursery and others will be given to friends. So when I sell, the garden will be rather depleted. Quite possibly, whoever buys the house may not be interested in my kind of gardening and might cast out all the things I loved. I couldn't bear to see that and shall be glad to be away when the house is sold.

August 22, 1940

I expect you kind folk over there may be wondering about us over here, especially if you've been listening to those lying Nazi broadcasts. I enclose an article about spurious British propaganda, so go let everyone know that they are not authentic no matter what the broadcasters say. I understand the Germans claim to have thoroughly damaged Sheffield. I must not give details, but Sheffield is still going strong.

The wind is dying down and the sky is clearing which I am afraid will mean an air raid tonight. Poor Doris heard from her home this a.m. (not in Sheffield) that a bomb which fell near to their house shattered the windows, brought down the sitting room ceiling, blew open the wash house door, and damaged the bathroom ceiling. Father, mother, and one sister retired to the cellar and were unharmed.

I have been tremendously fascinated by the searchlights. To me, it is very erie [sic] to hear German planes overhead and then to see the searchlights like long giant fingers which almost seem to tear at the clouds to find the enemy behind them. I had no idea searchlights were so bright. They even dim brilliant moonlight in their intensity. I should like to see one at the business end and see how they are worked. That wish is unlikely to be fulfilled while we are at war! Even an unimportant female like myself would soon be hurried off or more likely, be arrested long before I got anywhere near the thing!

A broadcaster told us a funny story today. A sailor on London navy patrol lost his identity card along with his yacht on the beach at Dunkirk while assisting in the evacuation of troops. He notified the authorities and received a note to the effect that 'it must be found'. Whereupon he rang them up and said that if it must be found, perhaps they would like to cycle over to Dunkirk and look for it themselves! Aren't clerks with a little authority fools at times?

August 23, 1940

I think one of the most evil inventions of man is the whistling bomb. It is terrible. The noise has the strange effect of making you feel as if you were going to burst, not only your ear drums and head, but the whole of your body. Whatever people with weak hearts will do, I cannot imagine. However brave you are, it has a terrifying effect. Of course, that's why it is dropped and we are all determined that we are going to bear those as best we may. The Nazis will not terrify us into submission as they are beginning to find out.

We have returned to high winds again, but they did not prevent 'visitations'. I got dressed but did not come downstairs as the bombing did not seem very near. When I get to the US it will be most unbelievable to be able to go to bed without being roused by enemy aircraft and bombs dropping. The joy of having as much butter and cream as I like will be almost too much for me! I am intimately fond of both! Mind you, this is not a complaint, because we are far from starving thanks to our incomparable Royal Navy, merchant navy, and wonderful air force. I personally eat more butter than average folk in normal times. It is wonderful how you can do without. It is really quite easy when you have to and everyone takes it as a matter of course and no one grumbles. When I mention food, please don't think I'm grumbling ever. I'm willing like everyone else to do with less as it is necessary and a help towards winning the war.

I'm going to have tea with an air raid warden's wife this afternoon and I fully expect to hear some funny incidents in the recent air raids. We always do have a good laugh when we meet. She is to take care of my canary when I come to startle the inhabitants of the United States of America. Dickey and she are great friends. She spoils him terribly and he just plays up to her. He will be in good hands. I am really rather afraid of the effects of the bombs dropping on him. I don't want him killed with a concussion nor do I want his cage blowing off the stand. I don't quite know the best thing to do with him now-a-days. I might not be able to get downstairs in time to do anything for him.

I had a hurried letter from J.M. He says they 'are having a lot of fun and very few leisure hours'. I don't think that is my kind of fun somehow! Our naval vessels seem to annoy Hitler. He's always trying to destroy them with little success so far.

I am told today that the German wireless said their airmen had damaged Sheffield works. Don't get worried about anything they say.

I do not feel I ought to give you any details, but I think I can safely say life in 'Old Smokey' (an affectionate nickname for Sheffield) is proceeding as usual and there are folk who, tired of getting up in the night watches and running to shelter, have simply put their beds in the air raid shelters, installed sundry comforts and betaken themselves there with the feeling: 'Now then, come on and do your worst!' The rest of us just carry on and are neither gloomy nor terror stricken. How the Germans dare describe the inhabitants of these islands as sitting cowering and terrified in their air raid shelters, sullen and angry with their leaders for rejecting the Fuhrer's peace offer, I do not know. That was promptly seized upon by our music hall and variety comedians. Friends will meet after an air raid with: 'Well, were you cowering in your air raid shelter?' That is met with: 'I laid down and had a little sleep to make up for what I lost the night before.' Does that sound to you Americans as cowering, sullen, and terrified?

August 24, 1940

As you know, they have started daylight air raids now and if they cannot get through in large numbers, they come singly not forgetting to bring and leave their bombs. A day or two ago during one of those aerial visits, a little girl of eight years was standing at the edge of the pavement absolutely terrified out of her wits. A workman on the other side of the road who had taken shelter, saw her and ran across the road, picked her up and ran to shelter. The bomber dived low and the gunner deliberately machine gunned them. The man was injured, but covered the girl with his body and managed to get to cover and safety. Then there are pacifists. The very word makes me choke with disgust.

Against that, a broadcaster told us a funny incident the other night. He along with some other golfers were enjoying a game when one or more enemy planes appeared. Everyone took what cover they could in the lee of bunkers or lay down in the bracken and heather. But some women players were well out on the course a good way from any cover, so they started to run but (to quote the broadcaster) 'They were built for comfort and not for speed and soon they dropped on all fours as the planes came lower. We who saw them were hoping that the gunners would not mistake them for a balloon barrage!'

August 25, 1940

I wonder what the Germans will say now! But please don't believe them. Mercifully last night's warning came before we were ready for bed and after one and a half hours the all clear sounded so we thankfully got into bed. The beauty of it all was that later on a terrific thunderstorm came on. I turned over and said to myself: 'That will put an end to any raids.' and went off to sleep again. Being waked by much heavier peals of thunder, I suddenly realized what it was! I only wish I could bound out of bed in a morning with the willingness and speed that I possess when danger calls me! Someone has been having a bad time and by the sounds the Germans met with a warm – nay hot – welcome. I am thankful to say that we are all right. If they hadn't sounded the all clear when they did, we should have been up for half the night! A friend whose husband is an air raid warden said I missed a most wonderful display of 'fireworks.' I am awfully sorry for the town or village that received the attack. I only hope the planes were brought down but of course even if I knew where they were, I shouldn't be allowed to say. But in the sky, things look nearer than they really are. Sound of course travels so far too.

I was tremendously amused the other day in the tram to hear a loud voiced woman describing to a friend her actions in a recent night raid. 'It came over our 'ouse several times' she asserted firmly. I might say the same, only I don't suppose it did anything of the kind. The heavy engines can be heard from far enough and I remember the visit of a zeppelin in the last war. According to all the people who said it went right over their house and they saw it, that old zep would have been touring over Sheffield for a week or two without stopping! When you remember the size of this city, even with modern speed capacity, it would hardly make such an extensive tour as all that in an hour or two. Did I tell you about a notice of recruiting in the last war? On the gate posts of one of the biggest public cemeteries was a poster: 'Wake Up! Your King And Country Need You!'

I have just seen a motorcycle corps of home guards pass (on a practice, I suppose) and saw a contemporary of mine whose son is in the army hanging onto his handlebars, looking straight ahead with grim determination on his face. I don't know how long he has been a motorcyclist, but I'm pretty sure he's never ridden anything since the days when he rode his wooden horse in his parent's home. The powers that be appealed to people to give their motorcycles for defense purposes. They appealed one night in 9 p.m. news. Next morning the police stations and recruiting offices were 'Soreyed out' with motorcycles (as we say in Sheffield.) Polite people like you would say 'snowed under' or 'completely overwhelmed'. That is the spirit of Britain.

I am going to send this letter off today while I am still frisky. We never know what might happen or where we may have to go. I personally have absolute and utter faith in our marvelous air force and our wonderful defences and I do not believe that many of us will suffer here. It is inevitable that some planes will get here, but they won't be invited to stay and, if possible, they will be despatched with all speed.

August 31, 1940

Oh, what a night we had! We have not had a full night in bed for a week! A warden friend of mine rang me up and told me not to go to bed. They had had a preliminary warning. We sat up until 1 a.m.

We had a raid that lasted six hours. I once said I could tell the sound of German planes from ours. Theirs sounds like the Nazis themselves, loud and explosive. What do they have to gain by slaughtering civilians wholesale? They seem to drop their bombs wherever they fancy.

A friend told me that people are taking their beds into the air raid shelters. I have brought chair beds into the downstairs for Doris and I for the bad nights. It is impossible to tell which are the bombs and which are the guns. The vibrations are about equal. When I'm lying there listening I wonder if there is anyone as frightened as I am! I need to find something else to do at those times. I used to knit, but the lack of sleep affected my ability to do that.

September 1, 1940

We had six hours of it again last night. I wish I were descriptive enough to get you to see it all. Doris and I lying on our camp beds, dressed, gas masks at the ready, and coats nearby in case of emergencies. The silence was broken by a loud zoom overhead. It was so appallingly close that I thought the evil thing came down in my precious little garden. I tried to remember what to do. Could I memorize the phone number to call? Could I find my sword stick in a hurry? Should I be able to capture the crew and hold them until help arrived? Above all, would I have the courage? Slowly I got up and felt for my slippers. It had to be done. One always has to face what has to be done. Somehow I got up. Suddenly there was a loud crash which shook us both. I realized that the bomb was a distance away – therefore the plane did not come into my garden so I lay down again. But I had such a feeling that it is rather selfish to hope I shan't be bombed, for if I don't get it, someone else will and it might be someone of more use to the community than I am. Sometimes there is such a row that I don't know which are bombs and which are guns!

It is terribly sad to think of those left homeless by the bombing. On Thursday a.m. people were very busy borrowing baby's feeding bottles, finding clothes and temporary homes for those who had nothing at all in the world but what they stood up in and at any moment it may happen to any one of us. Oh, I wish I could make you kindly folk in the US realize what it is like to be at war. What it is like to have air raids every night and have bombs rained on us indiscriminately. Now whatever you do, do not think I'm whining. Not at all. We are all in this together and together we stand. So do not be so misguided as to believe that England is being cowed and bombed into submission. We are being bombed, yes – cowed, no! Most of us are losing our looks, but we are all losing them together. Most of us are losing a good deal of rest, but we are all alike and Hitler will have to find some other way to beat us. We may suffer terribly, we may lose many things we value, we may lose loved ones, many of us have already lost our money, we may lose our homes, but we will not lose our Freedom, our Liberty, nor will we lose our dearly loved England.

September 2, 1940

We can very nearly set our watches by 'Jerry.' He comes zooming over promptly at the same time each night. But last night he suffered some delay or hindrance on his journey, for we went to bed in peace. However, during the night watches I was wakened by a bomb dropping and the hateful zooming overhead. I roused Doris and said we wouldn't get up and come down till we heard a bit more. (You see, we are already getting used to the bombing!) – but had better not go to sleep, just lie and listen, ready to spring out of bed, jump into clothes and downstairs when advisable. I was wondering if we were being wise, when suddenly I heard our Spitfires. Didn't Jerry's engines speed up! He was soon out of earshot. I smiled to myself in the darkness and turned over and went to sleep without another moment's anxiety. On many occasions, our Spitfires have attacked several enemy planes singlehanded. One of them once attacked nine and brought down seven. They soon run – or fly – away when the little Spitfires appear and the country has great faith in and a big affection for Spitfires. Everyone cheers up and feels 'now we shall be all right' when those elegant fast-moving planes heave into sight. I personally feel much safer when they tackle bombers than when the anti-aircraft guns start work, for the Spitfires can follow them up into the clouds and, of course, gunners cannot see behind the clouds.

I am told that the German broadcasters have been making the usual nonsensical extravagant claims about the damage they have done to Sheffield and other places. According to them, one of the coal mines in the village where Doris is from has been blown sky high. There are often nasty fogs there, but the sky never comes as low as that! The only damage done was a few broken windows in the office – even the office cat is uninjured.

We shall have an early autumn. In fact, it has already begun. I have only to turn my head slightly as I sit at my desk and I can see wonderful colouring. Exactly opposite the study window on the other side of the road is a sycamore tree. Framed by dark green leaves, it is a magnificent picture of gold and brown. Further to the left are some desdars with light green arms backed by somber yews with yellow beeches beside them, It is all so lovely that it is almost impossible that horrible bombing may take place in a few hours. So far, Jerry has not reached us by daylight.

NOTE: On 30 August, President Roosevelt signed an executive agreement that transferred fifty First World War era destroyers to Great Britain in exchange for the use of bases on British possessions in Newfoundland and the islands in the Caribbean. The arrangement allowed both nations to better defend themselves.

September 4, 1940

We are all very glad the US have granted us the 50 destroyers. I am not one of the people who thinks America should send an army. I feel material help of the kind we have been getting is more useful at present. I think your isolationists must be folk of a very low level of intelligence. Apart from anything else, and leaving help to Britain out of the question altogether, can't they see that what is happening to the whole of Europe will certainly happen to them if we are beaten? Hitler has repeatedly stated that world domination is his aim and even isolationists must admit that USA and South America form a considerable part of the world.

The fact that we might be beaten need not be considered. We are a tough lot. We have set our teeth and we are keeping on and I personally wouldn't be at all surprised if when Hitler finds he can't beat us, that he would turn his attention suddenly and swiftly to the Americans. I am not a politician, merely a woman who loves flowers and trees, and my views may not be held by anyone else – they certainly are not 'official'. But I repeat to American folk who are forbearing enough to read these words of mine: 'Prepare, Prepare, Prepare!' Hitler has to do something to save face among his own people, and when he has to do that, he always does something startling and unexpected.

It seems that 'Haw Haw' told us the other night that what we had had in Sheffield was a mere nothing, just a foretaste of what we are to get. That we are to get it hot and strong until we are wiped out. That is all right, but we also have something to say! Their aircraft by no means get things all their own way. I do wish you folk wouldn't get so worried about us. The direct descendants of Ananias have been appointed German news broadcasters. You know that. So when you hear that London is in ruins or that Sheffield was blown off the map, just say: 'We've heard those tales before.' I'll tune into the service at Westminster Abbey or the 9 p.m. BBC news or I'll write a friendly letter to so and so in Sheffield and she'll tell us how the moors are looking, if the heather is over and if the bracken has turned. She will perhaps describe the autumn color of the woods or tell us the latest air raid joke.

We have had the most terrible fires on the moors. I imagine prairie fires can be no worse. They dropped bombs into the fires one night. I thought the whole countryside was going up. They bombed the soldiers trying to put out the flames. The smoke is suffocating even eight miles away. The sky is brilliantly lit – most useful for the Jerrys. However, it won't be useful now! I think rain is blowing up. I hope so. I was literally nearly sick in the night with the smell of smoke. It was very trying. I don't know how folk who live nearer could live in it all. I am going out onto the moorland this afternoon to get some fresh air and livened up a bit.

NOTE: 'Lord Haw-Haw' was a nickname applied to the Brooklyn-born Irish American William Joyce, who broadcast Nazi propaganda to Britain from Germany during the Second World War. The broadcasts opened with 'Germany calling, Germany calling', spoken in an affected upper-class English accent. He was tried for treason and hanged by the British in 1946.

September 6, 1940

After a series of the most terrible explosions that I've ever heard in my life, it was pleasant to catch a bus soon after breakfast and get out onto the moors. We have some of the most beautiful country in England just round about Sheffield, and after the bus had droned on its way, we sat and looked at the magnificent view. All was peace and quiet except for the call of birds and now and again a lamb bleating. All around was purple heather just at its finest. The bracken was beginning to be tawny and the trees on the opposite hill were the yellow gold of limes, with the brown gold of beech, and the dark blue-green of the pines. In one direction were a few scattered farms, hundreds of years old, with fields of golden grain ready for the garnering. At our feet meandered a stream (usually a river full of trout) with willows dipping their overhanging branches into the now sluggish water. Big ashes cast their cool shadows across the shallow pools and smoke curled lazily from the farm chimneys. In the background rose blue shoulder after shoulder of the moorlands, getting paler and paler in the far distance. We sat and let the moor scented wind fill our lungs and blow away the cobwebs from our minds. In such a place it was easy to forget the broken nights, the dangerous darkness and war worriers. We felt rested and reassured. The mighty hills and rugged moors have stood for many thousands of years and will stand for many thousand more and will stand firm through all the machinations of war mongers, upstart dictators, and grasping blood-maddened men.

After a time, we wandered along a moorland path and picked cloud berries in berry and in flower. Also some of the pale bog heather and bell heather which reminds me so much of the highlands of Scotland. We might have been on a desert island instead of within a few miles of one of the world's great cities. I feel so refreshed mentally. How I wish I could live in the country altogether! Towns are all very well for use, but not for beauty. I feel I can face up to things better than I could before that short outing to the country. I think one can get things in their proper proportions so much better if one can see some natural beauty that is big and grand. Petty anxieties, big worries, and even the awful war seem less significant when one has looked upon such beauty as I saw this morning. Thank goodness Sheffielders have a great love for the country and anything on wheels that can be persuaded to turn is used to take them out where they can breathe pure, untainted air and see the wonders of natural beauty. I liked it so much the a.m. because the only other person to be seen except ourselves was an airman who left his motorcycle by the roadside and climbed up onto a rock a little way away from us and sat and drank it all in as if he couldn't bear to miss even a wisp of cloud. I must admit I like beauty spots to myself. I do not like crowds, except when I am lecturing!

September 8, 1940

Doris and I now prepare chair beds and a night light in my sitting room every night before we go to bed, so that directly we hear the 'Wailing Willies' we can dress hurriedly and just flop onto them and try to rest. Sitting up is too exhausting. Sometimes we hear the planes and bombs first – they are sufficient warnings in themselves! I now no longer feel so awful when I hear things begin to happen. If Willie wails, I think perhaps nothing will happen after all and if the bombs and fireworks have begun to play, I'm afraid I feel 'Oh, those beastly Germans again.' I hope they'll get what for – a horrible but popular Yorkshire expression. Most of us now feel more annoyance than fear. Though please don't think we are blasé about being bombed. We are angry at being continuously bombed and our plans interfered with on account of a bombastic blood-thirsty maniac desiring our extinction. Of course we are afraid too. I don't mind admitting it, but I am thankful I have trained my tummy to be British steady instead of sinking so that I can hardly stand upright. I'm afraid that on the last occasion, the explosions were so terrible that my chief thought at the time was a) where they were, b) hope that thousands of lives were not being lost, c) would this house stand the blasts if they came any further. It was only when all was quiet that I found my heart going fifty to the dozen and when I heard the German planes again, I felt rather sick. So you see I am not at all brave in reality. Most of my apparent courage is but Dutch courage after all. I don't mind in the least how I feel as long as I look calm! It does not do at all to appear scared (though everyone knows you are.) So long as you look cool, you don't upset other people.

There was a very fat woman getting dressed hurriedly in a nasty raid a short time ago. She bent down to put on her shoes and the blast from the bursting bomb blew her under the bed. Her husband and sons had to move the bed to get her out − she was stuck so fast! That is perfectly true − the girl who told me was told by the woman herself who thought it a huge joke which counterbalanced the fact that all the windows in the house were smashed and doors blown off. The thing she grumbled at − and she really did grumble about it − was at the piles of soot which covered everything. She didn't think one small chimney could hold so much. She did wish she had Hitler there − she'd rub his nose in it, she would!

Doris' mother had a narrow escape of being blown down the stairs and through the front door into the garden, but she hung onto the bannisters with all her might and so was saved.

NOTE: *Frustrated by the RAF's superiority over his air force and enraged at the British retaliatory bombing of Berlin in late August, Hitler ordered the Luftwaffe to destroy London. On 7 September, 300 bombers escorted by 600 fighters crossed the Channel to target London. Caught somewhat off guard at the targeting of their capitol, RAF fighters got involved in multiple dogfights in the sky over London. Parts of south and south-east London were devastated − 430 people killed and a further 1,600 injured, and firestorms ravaged that part of the city. The bombing of London continued for the next seventy-six nights.*

September 11, 1940

Today is a glorious day, stolen from the summer to put hope and warmth into us. I am now (2:30 p.m.) beginning to feel warm after being wailed out of bed in the early hours of the morning. It was cold and to make matters worse, bombs began to drop immediately and there was no time to dress before running downstairs. So we got really cold, and when two hours later we went back to bed I was unable to get warm. We should not grumble when we remember all the London folk are going through without any complaints. If Messrs. Hitler, Goering & Co. think the indiscriminate bombing of London is going to win the war by frightening us into submission, they've made another mistake. It is only making everyone angry. They deliberately bombed hospitals and a maternity home yesterday and our people will not take that filthy behaviour lying down. One of the hospitals was a children's hospital too. I understand that we here are on the murderer's visiting list to be attended to shortly. Well, that's as may be. But we have a Royal Air Force, a fact that Messrs. Murderers & Co. conveniently ignore when boasting of their intentions. I often wonder how the arch liars explain away the statement and promise that no British planes could ever penetrate the German defenses when the RAF has given practical demonstrations in plenty that they can get anywhere they like.

It is difficult – even for me – to write this afternoon. As Doris is out, I am writing in my sitting room window, a big one. The sun is pouring in and I am reveling in it. The sky is a very deep blue with beautiful banks of white clouds, some of which look like snow-capped mountains. The magnificent trees in the vicarage garden opposite are deep green, gold, and reddish brown. Just outside the window is what last winter left of my old English lavender hedge and a sweetbriar bush – both scenting air for yards as is my rosemary bush by the front door. The rose bed in the center is a mass of bloom and a flowering cherry with a terrible Japanese name that I dare not pronounce and cannot spell from memory is waving leaves of blood at me as a gesture of farewell. In front of it is a Japanese maple with finely cut foliage which has turned a glorious deep red, with fingertips of sealing wax red – the kind of colours that make you hold your breath and offer a prayer of thankfulness for the possession of your eyesight. I am glad my little garden is so lovely at the last, and I shall be able to take away with me many memories of beauty I have helped, even though imperfectly, to create. I like to see people stop as they go past, lean over the wall and sniff at the old fashioned scents and admire some of the more unusual colourings. It is difficult to think of war when you see lovely nature calmly working out her allotted plans. Though if I turn my head to one window, I can see balloons like silver fish against the blue sky. I much prefer the trees and blue sky, so do not turn away!

According to the 1 p.m. news, Londoners spent a fourth night in their air raid shelters. It has been very strange once or twice when listening to the wireless, to suddenly hear the London sirens wailing, warning everyone wherever the broadcast is coming from and yet we do not get a warning – mercifully – at that time. I thought all noise was excluded for the studios. On one occasion we heard bombs dropping and anti-aircraft fire, but the announcer carried on (it was a news bulletin.) Everyone in Britain is determined to carry on and let the Nazis burst themselves trying to stop us. They will tire first.

September 12, 1940

Last night we were wailed out of bed four times! I went into the city this a.m. and everyone feels that they must not grumble, for that is nothing compared to what London is suffering. The 1 p.m. broadcast told us about three boys of fourteen years of age who put out some incendiary bombs themselves, then tackled a big fire, helped to get out a number of cars first then set to with the hose. When the firemen came, the boys had prevented it spreading to other buildings. When they tried to stop the boys, they insisted on helping. The firemen were full of praise for them. When one of the boys' mother was spoken to about it and asked if she were not worried about him, she said: 'I don't mind where he is as long as he is doing his bit.'

I managed to get a chill in my back. The cold was surprisingly keen in the night and we had to run downstairs undressed, but hardly dare mention such a trifling thing in the face of what is happening elsewhere.

I went this a.m. to see about my passage to the US. I had no idea how anxious the British government is to keep me safe in the arms of authority! I look like I am having a real difficulty to get away. But as difficulties are made to be overcome, I shall have a good try. I like tackling difficulties. If I can get permission to leave the country there should be no further difficulties as transport to the US is available at certain times.

September 13, 1940

We had exactly ten minutes in bed last night! But I have fixed up two chair emergency beds in the sitting room and we lie down directly after we get downstairs. Bad sleeper that I am, I think I shall soon be able to sleep on the clothes line! It was awfully cold running downstairs in one's nightie. There was no time to dress first. Everyone is determined to stick it out until the bitter end and grumblers are not popular. Without wishing to be at all boastful, people are marvelous and there are heroes in the thousands. The most amazing deeds of heroism are performed by unexpected folk who behave as if they've done nothing at all.

September 16, 1940

Amazing! We had a whole night in bed. Just think of it. Something must have gone wrong with Hitler's plans. I sat up fairly late, as I did not see how we could escape aerial bombardment last night. The moon was almost full and the sky was cloudless – a perfect night to murder people from the heavens, as visibility was wonderful. But it cut both ways, as our defenders would be able to see the marauders clearly. True to their character, they would not come into the open where they could meet in a fair fight.

The bombing of Buckingham Palace has only infuriated Britons the more. When will the Germans learn that the King and Queen are one – or two – of us, and that they are not beings apart who have to go about in bombproof motor cars with body guards of troops to defend them. The King and Queen will not leave London until – or unless – its inhabitants do the same. Nor is the King abdicating – Why should he? I cannot see the reason for these wild statements in Berlin. If the King did abdicate, the war would continue. If every building in London is laid flat, the war will still go on. If everyone in London were to be killed, there are still some millions more of us to carry on the war. If the Houses of Parliament are bombed to bits, it will be a bit of a nuisance, but Parliament will still meet and the war will go on.

I am going to send this uninteresting epistle off today before Hitler begins his promised invasion. Frankly, his threats and 'promises' do not disturb us much. We are at war and war has come to Britain for the first time in centuries and we expect to suffer to some extent. We are bound to suffer, but that does not mean we have given in. We have plenty of food and are a long, long way from starving. Do let everyone know this. Everyone is cheerful and air raids are now taken as a matter of course – unpleasant episodes that are a hindrance, but which are accepted as part of the civilian's share of the Battle of Britain.

If the Germans land, I'm afraid they won't like Britain very much! Our leaders have never claimed that it would be impossible for enemy landings, as the jagged coastline is a terrific number of miles – I can't remember how many. No one need tell us what will happen to those who do land. Even the women folk would, if necessary, rise up with pitchforks, hoes, and other agricultural weapons and flay them. Indeed, one of our own airmen came down in a potato field and an army of land girls rushed with their forks, pitchforks, and hoes. It was with difficulty that he made them believe he was RAF! Then they couldn't do enough for him!

A few Nazi airmen landed by parachute in a place I had better not mention during the London raid and the attack on Buckingham Palace. The folk literally tore the German to pieces before the military could arrive to arrest them. This did not happen in London. All Britain is raging on account of the attack on London and on Buckingham Palace. I really don't know what would happen if they killed or injured the King and Queen. According to the rules of warfare, it isn't done to attack crowned heads, but Messers. Murders & Co. take no notice of the rules. If Hitler were caught, I cannot imagine what would happen. But he looks after his own skin along with Goering, Goebbels, Ribbentrop and all the other bullies.

I'm afraid this is all war, but it is really more interesting than my personal affairs.

September 20, 1940

I have been concerned in the most exciting doings! Oh, how I wish I could tell you all about it! What a story it would make after the war! I am quite unable to understand the mentality of people who live in a country like this, enjoy its freedom of action, liberty of thought, plenty of food and all the other things that go to make living in England such a privilege, and then betray the country that protects them. I would have no mercy on the women. They are a bit too fond of hiding behind their sex when it suits them. When it doesn't, they want to be the equals of men. Then let them be I say, and pay the same penalty for treachery as do men.

I wish you could see my fragrant evergreens on my desk. Every now and then I get a whiff of invigorating aromatic perfume. I shall miss all that terribly in America. I shall too miss the great joy of digging in the sweet smelling earth after rain and deciding that certain plants would look much better somewhere else, therefore putting them where I think they ought to be, regardless of the season!

We are now all agog for Hitler's invasion – ready and waiting.

September 22, 1940

After two or three nights in bed, we were fetched out just as I was getting pleasantly sleepy. I needed no siren – the bang of the bomb shot me out and I was groping for my clothes by the time the sirens were wailing. It was cold. I had had a hot bath and was nice and warm in bed. As we heard evidence of the Nazi activities, we grabbed necessities and ran downstairs without waiting to dress. I am wondering how many folk will get pneumonia or bad chills doing ditto and running out of doors to their shelters.

They are playing Rule Britannia on the wireless in a selection of regimental marches. Would not Hitler be annoyed when he says he rules the waves? If he does, why does he not invade us at once?

The Nazis seem to have a new kind of plane that sounds like a rattly old sewing machine about to fall to bits, as indeed any of his planes are if they come in contact with our RAF or anti-aircraft. The other night, when trying to go to sleep, I suddenly heard what sounded like the entire German air force overhead. (possibly there were three – probably only two!) In any case, there was a terrific row. I sat up in bed and wondered whether to get up without waiting for the siren. Then while I was thinking, all at once came the sound of our planes. It was almost amusing to hear the Germans put on all the speed they could and depart without even troubling to bomb us. I smiled to myself in the darkness and lie down in safety once more.

I wonder if less intensive raids indicate that the Germans are getting short of planes. I suppose their indiscriminate bombing of the east end residential part of London has been one to make the working class rise up and clamour for peace. The Germans seem utterly incapable of understanding the British mentality. Definitely they are very unlike us in enough ways to make it worthwhile to try to find out our reactions to certain events. But they do not understand finesse. Blundering, bullying, forceful methods are the only ones they are capable of practicing. If they did but know it, those are the very ways to make us all stand by each other. As for trying to kill the King and Queen, it has only made the whole country furiously determined to carry on to the bitter end. The trouble with Germany was that at the end of the last war we did not march in and too, they did not suffer from air raids, so they didn't know what they were in for. They know now.

No doubt you will know that Mr. Churchill will not allow reprisals as the bombed Londoners demanded. He pointed out that it would not help. At the moment we must concentrate on industries, their war appliances, and their navy so that they cannot attack. He has promised that the Germans will pay and pay in full. Mr. Churchill has promised and that is enough for all Britain. He is a statesman of his word. We are content to wait till such times it is deemed suitable to exact payment.

I had occasion to go into a bombed area the other day and I wondered at the destruction one bomb can do and I marveled thankfully at the comparative slight loss of life. I fail to see what military advantage can have been gained by damaging civilians and residential and shopping areas. A friend of mine who owns some property in the bombed areas has to replace 140 panes of glass. The blast from the bomb was the cause of the broken glass, as the bomb fell some distance away. It will be very good for those in the glass trade anyway. One of the women whose home was a mess of debris, a budgerigar (parakeet) in its cage on a table being the only thing left to her, said: 'Oh well, our men in the forces face worse than this. I'm still alive. I can get another home, but I can't get another life.' We have all been hunting up clothes and blankets. etc. ('clean and mended' according to official instructions) for those rendered homeless by the raids locally.

NOTE: *On 18 September 1940 a passenger vessel, the SS City of Benares, was torpedoed by a German U-boat in the North Atlantic and sank in less than thirty minutes. Onboard was a group of British children being evacuated from England to Canada. Seventy-seven of the evacuees were killed in the attack along with 183 others. The attack created increased rage in Britain.*

September 23, 1940

I have just been listening to the King's broadcast. We could hear the 'raiders past' signal being given in London while he was speaking.

All Britain has been shocked beyond expression by the torpedoing of the ship bearing those evacuee children. Just before the King spoke, there was a simple short service in memory of the killed and drowned children and of prayer for the sorrowing parents. We can hardly believe such an evil deed could be done even by Germans. I pity any Nazi airman who has to make a forced landing tonight or tomorrow if there is no military at hand to protect them.

This afternoon I had a visit from an air raid warden saying that my name had been suggested as possibly being willing to allow this house to be used in any way that might be necessary in case of bombing in the immediate neighbourhood and that I myself might be willing to assist anyone in misfortune. Of course I gladly consented. This house has always been a sort of unofficial ambulance station, as this hill is very steep and cyclists have had some nasty spills just outside the gate. I shall have to do what I can till the services arrive and of course I've always been willing for anyone to come in if necessary in an air raid. So far no one has found it necessary to do so. Anyone who wouldn't help just deserves to be bombed themselves.

I have had quite an amusing time trying to get my Exit Permit before I can get a passport. (I was solemnly reminded that levity would be frowned upon by the Powers That Be!) I have had to give your address as my ultimate destination and it is quite possible that they might write to you. I am supposed to give proof of my lecture tour. As no one will book me before I get to the USA, that part of it is going to cause me trouble. But as I've said before, I enjoy overcoming difficulties. I only hope the Atlantic will be cleared of U-Boats before I sail. I doubt very much if I shall really get off in November. I am going to try anyway, but don't expect me to be punctual! No doubt there will be all kinds of aggravating delays. The U-Boat difficulty I should not enjoy.

September 26, 1940

I have been buzzing round after my passport etc. How spies ever get out of the country, I cannot imagine when honest folk with nothing to hide have so much difficulty!

September 28, 1940

I have spent a good deal of time running about after my 'exit permit' before I can get a passport. I have actually registered with either the Cunard or White Star line for a berth if I can get permission to leave the country. So I am beginning to feel that perhaps it won't be just a dream after all and that sometime before my hair is snow white, I may turn up in New York. I have resorted to a little wire pulling in order to get away. Now that I have taken the plunge, I want to be off at once. I'm like that. I interviewed the bank manager and arranged for various things to be done in my absence. He says don't build on getting there quickly, as a customer of theirs has been waiting for six weeks for permission to go to India to marry one of the officers there. But I should imagine there are more boats to the USA than to India in these days.

We are getting quite used to disturbed nights and I am trying to learn to distinguish between the sound of bombs and the sound of anti-aircraft fire. To know our guns are banging away as well as the bombs is very heartening. It makes me at any rate feel safer. Although someone told me after a recent air raid: 'the shrapnel from our guns fell on our roof like rain.'

We are now reduced to two ounces of butter per week instead of four ounces. I have decided that when I have it for breakfast (which won't be very often) I shall put the portion I am allowed all onto one piece of bread and then I shall forget I am rationed! We shall not suffer from bilious attacks because of eating too much butter! We are to have our meat ration per head raised by four pence each. That is, we can each have fourpenny worth of meat per week. I hope they won't reduce tea and sugar again. But if by so doing the war would be over sooner, every one of us would cheerfully accept the ruling.

J.M. has just had three days leave. He spent the afternoon with his 'sea mammy' and I did enjoy his visit. Doris took a photo of both of us in the garden. He should have had three weeks leave, but all leave in the forces is cancelled in preparation for invasion or other of Hitler's antics. He did not leave bombing attacks behind unfortunately, though think he was quite safe at his home. He should be back on duty once more. He is twenty-one on October 3rd. Such a pity he could not be at home for it. He told me that when the newspapers arrived from you, the trouble was that everyone on the ship wanted to borrow them before he'd been able to see them himself. Several things that I have sent him have never arrived – a letter describing D.W. and S.T.'s wedding, some socks and a photograph – all my time knitting wasted. However, I don't want to grumble. I've made up my mind never to utter a grumble till the war is ended. As a woman whose home has been bombed to bits and had nothing but what she stood up in said: 'Well, we've got our lives – that to old 'Itler' and I'm afraid she made a rude face. The

Germans may ruin our homes, bomb our beauty spots, and cause us some inconvenience, but they won't crush our spirits. It's born in us to be more determined than ever when we are wrongfully treated or up against things.

The torpedoing of the ship with the children evacuees roused the country to a wild fury, as did the bombing of the east end of London. If the Nazis hoped that that action of theirs would make the working folk clamour for peace, then another of their hopes is shattered for the east enders say: ''Itler isn't going to turn us out, not likely. This is where we live and here we stay' and they do — to the hindrance of those deputed to care for the homeless.

Last night I heard part of a German broadcast saying that the stories of the RAF successes in Germany were all lies on the part of the British government. That we did not have enough air raid shelters for people and that the British working class was not allowed to use air raid shelters. Did you ever hear such lies? Now THAT would cause the working classes to revolt! If it were true, then England would deserve to lose and be crushed. I think such a lot of their stories are so silly, too silly to believe. If they want to use lies as a form of propaganda, I wonder with all their efficiency that they cannot think of more convincing statements.

Do you know the Shetland knitted goods? They are lovely and I wondered if Barbara wanted one of their hand knitted jumpers. What colour does she like? If the woman I know has not been killed and Barbara would like one, I will ask her to knit one for me and bring it over with me. Some of the Fair Isle patterns are said to date from the 16th Century and Spanish Armada days. Some of the moors were on the Spanish ships and they taught the designs to the Shetlanders when their ships were wrecked on the islands. I never buy Shetland knitted goods from ships. I prefer to deal with the knitters themselves. I've promised myself one of their shawls which are like cobwebs, so fine that they will pass through a small ring and yet are beautifully warm.

One of Doris' sisters is a nurse in a north London hospital. In a recent letter she said that air raids were practically incessant. She is on night duty and one night the nose of a shell came through the window passing over her head and missing it by about an inch. Another time when she went out of doors a piece of shrapnel scraped down the side of her leg tearing her stocking to shreds. What a narrow shave that was! The casualties are very brave. She said one man, who is badly injured, keeps imploring them to let him show them where his wife and mother-in-law are. The house is bombed to bits, but he keeps saying: 'I know just where they are. I can take you to the very spot. Do let me go.' No one dare tell him they are both in the hospital mortuary.

Doris has gone into the city to help her other sister buy her wedding outfit. Doris is to be bridesmaid and has got a very pretty frock with my aid and abetting. It is a very unusual shade of mulberry pink. Alice, Doris' sister, is a nurse at our biggest Sheffield hospital and is a very nice girl indeed. I shall be glad to see Doris back, as we may expect an air raid anytime now. I never go out after blackout time and yet the day is rushing by.

Most folk seem to think that we are next on the list after London. So sincerely hope Silver Hill Nurseries will escape Nazi attention. That is where most of my plants will be kept while I am away. Twice I've seen a plane (British) flying so low over the nurseries I thought it was trying to find a landing place, but it flew away fortunately. I think it would be a good plan to bring Barbara back to England with me and she could go to one of our foremost universities. What do you say? I have applied for two years leave of absence, if the USA can bear me for two years!

September 29, 1940

It has occurred to me that you might be interested in an account of the procedure during air raids. Works, police, army, air raid wardens, hospitals and other important bodies receive a preliminary warning that hostile aircraft are within a certain radius. When this happens, all vehicular traffic puts out lights with the exception of the minimum possible for safety. Then sometimes the aircraft go away or more often, they get here. When we get the Wailing Willies (now and again we sometimes get the bombs and no warning is needed!) everyone takes cover except the important services who have to see that everyone else is safe. As soon as a bomb is dropped, the air raid warden and police report it – that makes me want to laugh, as though everyone in a radius of many miles had not heard it and probably had their house shaken by it! Then ambulance workers, fire and salvage workers dig out the ruins and rescue parties at once set to work to find those buried in the debris – bombs probably falling all around them while first aid posts and hospitals stand by ready to receive casualties.

A man told me after an unpleasant raid that he was so busy that he really literally did not notice the bombs falling round him. All he thought about was could he get the injured women out in time to save their lives. You have no idea of the queer feeling it gives you to know there is the 'purple warning'. Purple warning is not a siren, but only given to workers, hospitals, police, etc. to indicate enemy in district. I lie in bed trying not to strain my ears, but my ears, like horses, seem to instinctively prick up at every sound. I have just been examining them in the glass to see if they are acquiring a permanent prick. Then comes the sound of the plane apparently, but probably not, overhead. Sometimes he is circling over for a long time and finally departs when my stomach returns to its normal level and my ears cease to prick. Unfortunately, he does not always go quietly, he is apt to leave a memento – one no one wants. Most of us are so used to the awful wail of the sirens that we no longer feel that our last moments have come. Rather we do feel that the last moments of our attackers have come, as indeed they have thanks to the RAF.

When bombs drop my first anxiety is where did they drop and is everyone safe? – especially personal friends.

I almost think that delayed action bombs are the worst. Often their whereabouts are unknown or uncertain until they go off. When that happens, all argument ceases! If it is known where they are, then the authorities take all possible precautions – clear everyone away within a given radius, sometimes they try to remove it, sometimes they don't. If they don't, it removes itself all in good time along with tons of masonry, earth, steel girders, etc. etc. – anything in its environment.

September 30, 1940

Strange I should have mentioned delayed action bombs. For about 6 a.m. there were some terrific explosions which sounded like delayed action bombs. I think it was not an actual raid as there were no planes and no sirens. But the whole city woke with the noise. It shook the house.

The BBC has inaugurated a new broadcasting service for news and programs with USA. They have asked listeners here to send the addresses of those who would be interested in the US and the BBC itself will send them the times, etc. So you should then be able to get authentic news. I'm sending your address, Mrs. Ronin's and Mrs. Searles'. Let me know if you hear from the BBC please.

October 2, 1940

I am off fish at present. There are so many dead Germans being caught in the fishing nets and washed up on our shores, that I don't fancy it very much.

We have had some horribly gloomy almost foggy days. I never know whether to be thankful for fog or not as the Germans can get to where they want within a mile or two by compass and as they have no compunction where they drop their bombs, good visibility might or might not be an asset to either side. It reminds me of the tormenting question of my school days. 'Would you rather be as silly as you look or look as silly as you are.' No answer being really satisfactory!

Doris is going out this afternoon so will bring this epistle to the Americans to an end and she can post it.

I am much afraid I shall not get away in November. There is so much to do and I have to wait my quota for the shipping accommodation. I do hope the submarines will mind their own business while I am crossing. Apart from being torpedoed, even if I am saved, I do not want to lose my lantern slides, my manuscripts and certain books of reference. Some of them are out of print and obtained in the past with some difficulty. However, I must take the risk.

It is almost time for the 1 p.m. news so must depart to the culinary regions and see if all is well with the lunch.

Yours cheerfully (like everyone else in England).

October 6, 1940

Since I last wrote I have sat in the cockpit of a German Messerschmitt 109 and flapped its wings, wagged its tail, shot its machine gun and cannon and manipulated its wireless. No, no, no – I've not turned traitor and betrayed my dear old England! Nothing of the kind! A Messerschmitt shot down 'somewhere in England' is on view in Sheffield, the charge for admission is for the Newspapers Comforts fund and the charge for sitting in it is double the admission! I have since wondered what I must have looked like as we had to climb in and out, there was no door. I never noticed the crowd I was so interested. When sitting in it, I wondered what the crowd would do – to say nothing of myself – if I touched a button that started the thing and I flew out over the crowd and up into the sky! Of course it was well out of action and had been burnt as well as knocked about by our RAF. I thought about how very lonely up in the sky all alone in a thing like that. The beast had two white marks on its tail to show it had shot down two of our planes. It was wonderful to me to see how easily the whole thing worked. There was a loose 'stick' like a brake handle in a motor car that guided the plane. In the stick were knobs for firing two machine guns and one cannon, just at hand were the wireless buttons. To think what brains must have been necessary to concoct such a machine. What a pity brains are used to devise death dealing instruments rather than life giving.

October 8, 1940

Such a nice long kind letter from Mrs. Searles this morning. Written on August 28th it has taken about six weeks to get here. But what on earth has happened to you? There is a terrific gale blowing. I hope the chimney pots will stand it. The wind is howling like banshees and leaves are being driven off the trees flying like snow flakes. This will put 'paid' to all hopes of any more garden flowers. In spite of stout stakes everything is laid flat.

October 12, 1940

I have had an enquiry from Brooklyn Botanic Garden re my fees. They are having an anniversary celebration next September and consider inviting me to speak.

You will have heard that the Nazis bombed St. Paul's cathedral. I am so sorry about it, but I have never had the affection for St. Paul's that I have for Westminster Abbey. I love every stone in the Abbey. St. Paul's is, of course, not as old as the Abbey by hundreds of years and I always feel it is too continental and I loathe all the statuary about. Its outward appearance is dwarfed on account of being so built up. But, of course, it is a magnificent place and a national historic building, beloved by countless Britons the world over. But I personally would plump for the Abbey every time!

Last night's news told us they'd hit Canterbury cathedral, another of our oldest cathedrals. I have a copy of the original plan of the herbarium, the only plan of any abbey herbarium known to be in existence in Britain except Branchiel Abbey built in the 12th century, about half an hour's walk from here and where I am hoping in favorable times to lay out an Old World garden on the lines of the original. It was a great joy to me to handle the really old plans by Branchiel. The parchment is discolored with age, but the drawings are quite distinct and easily followed.

I suppose we can expect our beautiful buildings and our beauty spots to be the special targets for Nazi bombers. Men who will deliberately bomb hospitals and ambulances cannot be expected to reverence cathedrals and churches. Sir Christopher Wren rebuilt St. Paul's after the great fire in the 16th century and also built a few more London churches, one at least of which has been bombed.

I am going out to tea this afternoon with a friend whose brother was knocked down by a tram car in the blackout, they had to get jacks to lift the tram up in order to get him from underneath. It is just marvelous that he is alive. His head and eye were injured the most. The doctor says he must stay in bed but he waits till the doctor has been and then gets up, and goes downstairs and sits by the fire. His wife can do nothing with him. So like a man!

A friend of mine has been having an exciting time. Time bombs were dropped in their road and opposite to them on some golf links – somewhere in England. They get about five raids a day and I don't know about the night raids, think they are a continuous performance. No one was admitted to the road and the inhabitants hoped for the best. Eventually the bombs were removed by the right people instead of the wrong people being removed by the bombs! But unfortunately that does not always happen.

We still have enough to eat and plenty. I hope by the time this reaches you you will have heard from the BBC about their new broadcasting arrangements to the USA and then you will get first hand news. Be sure to listen to it and when you know the exact times, tell all your friends about it, please.

I am having considerable difficulty in getting permission to leave the country. I wrote the officer commanding some barracks not too far away to say I would be pleased to entertain four soldiers every Thursday evening. I'm now waiting to see what – if anything – turns up! I'm trying to think up all the lively tricks and card games I can.

Did you hear Princess Elizabeth's broadcast on Sunday? I was so anxious to hear it I wrote the time on a piece of paper and propped it by the clock on the mantlepiece. A friend who had visited the States' universities a few years ago came to tea, to tell me 'all about America' and we said whatever happened we mustn't miss Princess Elizabeth. Quite near the end of the broadcast we remembered it!! I switched on at once but we only heard a little of it.

I wonder what Greece and Turkey will really do. In the last war all the men said that the Germans, though nominally Christians, were dirty fighters, but that the Turk, though a Moslem and a deadly fighter, was a gentleman. The Turks did not do nasty tricks when taking prisoners, or when surrendering themselves. They had a great reputation for being clean fighters.

Most of the German airmen who are taken prisoners here in England will not believe that the Germans have not invaded us. They insist that London is a smouldering heap of ruins and that we are about to surrender and that we are starving. They are utterly amazed when they see the food they are allowed and when they find they have to travel by train to their prison camp they are speechless with surprise. They have been told that all our railway communications have been destroyed. They have not. Neither has our morale. A friend was telling me the other day she had occasion to go into an area that had been bombed. The particular street she was in consisted of tiny shops, cottage shops we call them. I don't know whether you have anything like them, America being the Land of Bigness in everything! But they are very small, in a working class district, often the front room of a tiny house. The windows had, of course, all been smashed, and since repaired. There was a notice upon one repaired window. 'Business as usual. Try again, Old Nasty', 'Old Nasty' being a popular nickname of Hitler's.

The trees are all looking so lovely just now and the road is carpeted with gold, beautiful to look at, but treacherous to walk on in this damp weather. My garden is in a dreadful state. I have neglected it shamefully, there has been so much to do. I made some sage jelly the other day, to eat with pork, if we get any! or duck. There are delightful things to make with herbs out of the garden. Did I ever tell you how to make mint pastry? It is a Yorkshire recipe. Make some good short pastry and cut into rounds, on half a round place some dried currants, brown sugar, a tiny dab of butter and some chopped mint (apple mint is extra good). Then wet the edges, fold over the half and press together, prick with a fork and bake in a hot oven. Eat hot or cold. We call them pastries. You will perhaps call them turnovers.

October 19, 1940

I have just received a letter from the other sailor to whom I write. He went over to Canada to fetch the destroyers from US. He writes the most delightful letters. He gave a very amusing description of his first – and only – flight in an airplane. In Canada they took him up and turned him upside down. To quote his own words: 'Gosh! Old Mother Earth commenced to dash around in places it never ought to have been. The sky also began to gyrate in a most terrific manner … To cut a long story short the earth slowed up sufficiently enough for us to land on it.' It seems they never charged him anything! I always said he could get things by smiling that other people would have to pay through the nose to get! He is like that and a very nice fellow, indeed.

I am beginning to look through and collect things ready for my trip to US if I can get permission to leave the country. It is very difficult to do. I cannot imagine how spies and undesirables ever manage it, when straightforward folk have so much difficulty.

I wonder if you have yet heard from the BBC about their US broadcasts. I hope you will listen if you do. I wonder how you like the cartoons in our papers? Some of them are so good. I can't think how they can think of some of them. They are really apt and clever.

October 21, 1940

Thanks so much for the August 19th number of the *Time* and the picture supplement from the *New York Times*. I always enjoy seeing it and I send it to J. M. when I've finished. But I am so disappointed that there is no letter from you. I just feel I should like a cheery letter from everyone in America who is sensible enough to wish Britain well in her struggle with brute force and evil.

The map of the 'Midlands' in *Time* interested me. I should have been less interested had the whole thing been more correct! It is a week today since I posted you an air mail letter. The girl at the post office told me that someone received an air mail letter that took thirteen weeks to reach her! I hope mine will be more prompt, as business appointments in the shape of lecture bookings cannot be kept open indefinitely awaiting my replies.

I am very anxious about friends up and down the country. Some live in badly bombed areas and I cannot expect letters after every raid to say they are safe. It is a horrible feeling when lying awake in the night to hear distant gunfire and bombs exploding. You have no idea where it is, as it is amazing the distance that the sound of gunfire and bombs can travel. One day when this house – and most of Sheffield – shook with the force of explosions, I thought some armament factory must have blown up and was very uneasy until I learned that the bombs were dropped in fields about twenty miles away, killing only cattle. Bits of dead cow, a horn, an odd leg, part of a cow's body, etc., were picked up about a quarter mile away from the explosion. I could not help thinking what on earth would have happened if the armament works had been hit. It is a horrible sound to hear the German planes circling 'round and 'round. Those who know about such things tell me that they sound overhead when they are perhaps as far as twelve miles away. But twelve miles in the air, with no corners to turn, is mighty near, and far too close for comfort. Besides, unfortunately, they are not always twelve miles away!

I do not describe or enumerate the air raids, because after all, one air raid is pretty much like another, the only difference being in its severity or mildness. Mildness is quite the wrong word to use. I will say instead in its severity and deliberate brutality. I like the way the Germans squeal now the RAF is bombing Berlin. Why shouldn't they know what bombing is like? They never had a bomb in the last war. If they had, they would never have allowed the upstart Hitler to lead them into war. After all, the RAF does aim at military objectives and does not deliberately bomb hospitals, ambulance trains and schools, nor does it machine gun women and children.

I wonder if you heard Winston Churchill on Monday night. I do hope so. When he spoke in French, the Germans jammed it. If their own reports are correct, why be so terrified that the German people should hear foreign broadcasts. In Britain we are at liberty to listen where we like, in the same way as you are.

We still have plenty of food and we are still not a beleaguered island.

October 24, 1940

Last night was a fairly peaceful night. It was terribly dark. I don't see how any plane could find its way even by compass. Today it is bitingly cold. These northeast winds do not please me at all. They go right through you. We have had a great deal of fog and most abominable weather generally. The weather has always been a great standby to those who feel it necessary to 'make conversation' on all possible occasions and a source of great comfort to grumblers. But now-a-days, the worse the weather, the better our safety from air attacks. Whoever would have thought that our English weather reviled by all visitors to these islands, endured by its grumbling inhabitants, sought by some migrant birds and responsible for some of the loveliest gardens in the world would be hailed with joy when it was at its very worst? Hitler has accomplished an extraordinary feat! Britons no longer grumble at the fog!!! Indeed, we don't grumble at all in these days: Why should we? We are better off than any other European nation, thanks to our navy and air force. We have enough to eat, wear and burn. No one is likely to be short of coal for want of supply. There are plenty of clothes in the shops for those who wish to buy, there is plenty of food. There is also plenty of water! Thanks to the recent heavy rains. The fire brigades should not be short when dealing with incendiary bomb blazes, etc.! So even the weather helps us. Hitler and his evil gang with all their devilish inventions, secret weapons and the like, cannot control the elements. Praise be!

When Doris calls me in a morning and says 'There's a letter from America for you' the day begins so brightly, however foggy and dark the outlook.

My new war work is quite interesting. I wrote the commanding officer of a camp telling him I would be pleased to see four men each Thursday evening at 6 p.m. As the clock whirred to chime the first stroke of six, four airmen walked up the path. I was in what Doris calls a 'twitter' for fear they'd be bored stiff and by the time they arrived, was heartily wishing I had not been so rash. However, most people like to come again when they have once been, so I went into the hall to welcome them. It was pouring so their thick army coats had to go into the kitchen to be dried. I thanked

Providence for my 'gift of the gab' which has so often gotten me into trouble, but which equally often has been a godsend, and talked hard for a few minutes. However, later we played various card games and they thawed considerably. One of them was – I am sure – the camp humorist. He was most amusing! He always had something funny to say. I cannot afford elaborate meals, to say nothing of the rationing, so I only provided a simple one, but they seemed to enjoy it. I asked a very attractive nineteen-year-old 'adopted' niece in. She could not get here before 8 o'clock, but my goodness, how they brightened up when she came!! One of them was nearly old enough to be her father, but he brightened up too, and teased her about her play. The end of it was – they all but asked outright to be allowed to come again! It was very awkward as they were being moved yesterday further out, and the officer would send four men from the next lot that came to camp, so I just asked them for Tuesday evening and trusted that I should be able to find refreshments for them, plus the other four next Thursday.

What devilish trick do you think the Germans are up to now? You kindly folk in America would never think of it. In France many land mines were laid to stop the advancing Germans who, now that they have subdued France, have dug them up, attached detonators to them and dropped them from their planes on to Britain. The damage they do is therefore more widespread, as a bomb crater is usually a few feet only in width and depth, but these things are awful, tearing up the place where they fall terrifically and cause tremendous havoc.

Last night we had the earliest raid we have yet had. Thank goodness I was indoors and had no visitors to consider either!

Your letter had not been opened by the censor. Do tell me if at any time they censor anything I say. I do not want to say anything I shouldn't, but it could easily be done unintentionally.

So Greece has entered the fray. Let us hope the Italians will not overrun her like the Germans have done other countries. No wonder Hitler and Mussolini want Spain to help them. I must have a good look at the Atlas. Some people have a map of Europe pinned on the wall. I don't want my walls spoiled by a reminder of poor, unhappy Europe. There is enough of war in the papers, the news, the magazines, the films, the shops and in life without looking at a map of unfortunate countries who hadn't the sense to prepare well beforehand so as to put up a good resistance. Poland was the best resister. I suppose by tomorrow – perhaps sooner – Turkey will be in it too. I have been baking this morning in preparation for the airmen tomorrow night. I shan't be able to do that often on account of the fat rationing and the sugar.

October 30, 1940

Last night the airmen came to see me. One of them lives in an important east coast town. He told me the Germans had been dropping land mines, which they had dug up in France, attaching detonators to them. They are terribly deadly things. The destruction they cause is far worse than air bombs. So far they have not penetrated far inland with them. I believe they are too heavy to carry far.

Doris's brother-in-law was torpedoed on a troop ship, but fortunately he was among the saved and unwounded.

An acquaintance told me of a London woman who has been evacuated to a less troubled area. She thinks it's awfully quiet and hates it, so she is going back to London 'where she can see what is going on'. That is, I suppose, very fool hardy, I must admit that, but is the general spirit prevailing. No one wants to leave London, or to run away even from such appalling horrors as have been happening. In fact, folk mostly say: 'I'm not going to let Hitler drive me away, no fear!' And drive them away he does not, till he kills them or maims them dreadfully. Most of the Sheffield evacuees are back again now and tiny tots even know the ominous sounds of enemy planes and Wailing Willies.

Letters From Sheffield To Penn Yan Reveal Life In England During War

(Life in England during these war days—with its fear of air raids, its blackouts. its rationing of bacon and butter, its censored news and propaganda—is pictured in the following excerpts from letters written to Mrs. Charles Beaumont of 314 Clinton street, Penn Yan, during the past few months by her cousin, Miss Winifred M. Granville of Sheffield, fifth largest city and a leading industrial center on the isles. Miss Granville is an authority on trees, flowers and Old-World gardens, having lectured and written widely on this interest. She anticipates a lecture tour in this country soon. William Milispaugh, whose father, Levi, ran a wagon shop in Branchport years ago, runs a steel mill in Sheffield, England.—Editor.)

and I literally could not see the door step although I was standing on it, or my handkerchief which was white. I do not remember such darkness. But we are thankful for it. It is protection.

Sheffield is an armament city. Armor plates, shells, steel plates for the battle ships and submarines, etc., are all made here. We are (like Jerusalem) built on hills and all round and in the city there are anti-aircraft guns. If we know where they are we are asked not to tell even our best friends as there are spies here. They will get them sooner or later we know, but they can be

(Continued on page ten)

Article from the 25 April 1940 issue of the Chronicle-Express, *Penn Yan, New York, accompanied by a picture of Miss Granville. (Jane Beaumont photo: Yates County History Center, NY)*

Heinkel He 111 bombers during the Battle of Britain. (Public Domain)

Trying on gas masks in Sheffield, 1939. (Sheffield Libraries and Archives)

Air-raid damage along the High Street in Sheffield. (Mirrorpix)

Bomb damage near the Court House (Old Town Hall) in Sheffield. (Family of photographer Frank H. Brindley)

Making the injured comfortable after the Blitz in Sheffield's city centre. (Sheffield Newspapers Ltd)

German Messerschmitt 109 plane brought down in Sheffield, September 1940. (Sheffield Libraries and Archives)

Royal visit of King George VI and Queen Elizabeth to Sheffield after the Blitz, January 1941. (Sheffield Libraries and Archives)

NOTE: At this point authorities began to censor Miss Graville's letters, although somewhat sporadically. Hence the blacked out words in some of the letters that follow.

November 4, 1940

Oh, how it rains! I wonder if it will ever be sunshiny again. Last night was the first time for fifty-six nights that London had no air raid alarm. There was a little enemy activity over the country, but not much. The eldest daughter next door has lost her husband after nine months of marriage. He, his mother and father were all killed by a direct hit from a bomb which crashed straight through the house in London. The rescue squad was unable to get to them for a fortnight and the mother had her thimble on her finger and the needle in her hand when they found her all that time later, just as though she were still sewing. The telegram announcing the funeral did not arrive here until the day after it was all over. There had been so many telegrams to send that the post office was swamped, So the poor girl had no one of her own with her at the funeral. They are all very much upset.

The more I think of it the more astonished I am at the writer of that news cutting you sent. It was very far from being the first time enemy planes got here. Indeed, at this end of the town many were without water after the first time they came. We had water, but it was black mud. The water carts had to deliver water once a day for two days only as a ▆▆▆▆▆▆ the reservoir itself had been untouched. If that had burst, thousands of people might have been drowned. It was horrible stuff that came through the pipes, but I felt that I just didn't care a bit as no lives had been lost. The bomb fell very near to some friends of mine. Another time a number of ▆▆▆▆▆ were dropped in another part. You see ▆▆▆▆▆▆ is such a huge place that as nothing in detail is broadcast or printed, this district might have an awful time and somewhere else be untouched, and other districts might not know we had been hit at all. I have not given any details about raids in these letters as I did not want to say anything I should not. I am giving your address to friends so that if I am bombed, they can let you know. I devotedly hope there will be no need to let you know!

One of the airmen who came last Thursday said he had seen a ▬▬▬▬ German planes at once in the sky. He said it was just like a cloud of flies 'round a horse's head and the noise was awful. Another man from an important east coast town described a land mine being dropped onto his town. One minute there were houses, gardens and streets, the next minute nothing but debris and the windows of ▬▬▬▬▬ smashed to atoms ▬▬▬▬. Houses nothing but a heap of ruins and the occupants that were still living homeless, having lost everything except the clothes they stood up in.

I expect I may hear more when the men come Thursday, but I make a point of not discussing the war at all if I can help it. The men are off duty and have come to have a jolly time, if possible, so I do not ask questions or encourage war talk.

November 6, 1940

I understand from the 1 p.m. news that President Roosevelt is likely to be elected again. I do not consider American elections are any business of ours, but naturally we are interested, tho' it is not for us to make comments, it being a domestic affair so to speak. What a complicated affair your presidential election seems to be. We have a direct vote for our MP and there it ends as far as we are concerned with voting.

The Greeks appear to be holding their own. I heard in the 1 p.m. news that Italian planes bombed a Jugoslavian town. Italy said that they were Greek or British and Berlin said it was definitely established that the planes were British!! It's likely, isn't it? As though when most of Europe is under the heel of Hitlerism we should deliberately bomb a neutral country! I suppose they found some papers in a train establishing our guilt. That is the usual German method. Their discovery of papers of that sort is unusually marvelous even for Germany!! There must have been some very careless people in charge of these wonderful documents!! I wonder how much was the reward for – writing – them!!

I shall soon become web footed and mouldy. Oh! the rain! Tomorrow night is my air night again. How quickly the Thursdays come 'round! I am getting used to the invasion in my quiet life now.

Last week I went out to tea – tea again! – to see a friend who allowed me to miss the bus, her clock being wrong and I was unsure of the bus times. So I decided to walk some distance and catch another bus. To my astonishment I discovered the 'purple' was on. That is a silent preliminary warning when buses and trams run without lights with the exception of a tiny front one low down and all motor cars run with so little light you don't know they are there till they are practically on the top of you. I did not like it a bit. I've never been out in 'the purple' before, but by the time I boarded the bus it was off. But I had not been home long before it was on again. It is sometimes on and off eight or ten times in an evening. It does not always develop into a raid, thank goodness. But all who are out of doors soon get to know and if they are wise they make tracks for home. I can easily know any time when it is on, as I watch for the buses passing the house and now that the trees are bare I can see across to a main road and can see the trams passing at night, if it is all serene. 'The purple' means that enemy planes are within a certain radius, I don't know how near. I was told but have forgotten, but near enough to need caution on the part of everyone with their feet on solid earth! Sometimes we can hear the planes. It is an eerie feeling to stand at the door, see buses passing in the purple and all the time to hear the beastly things zooming up above and unable to see where they are. I always hope so terribly hard that no male passerby will light a match for his cigarette or flash his torch, for the light would be seen and we should never be seen again! For wherever they see a light the Germans drop their bombs in this part of the world, that is. So far we have had no daylight raids here. They were here before it was quite dark the other day. Such cheek! But that particular plane was shot down. There is a German bomber here on show this week. I don't know whether I shall get to see it or not.

In these days I often wonder what has happened to the few foreigners who have previously come my way. I met a perfectly delightful Roumanian girl about a couple of years ago. A friend brought her to see me. She spoke very good English. I think, too, of the Hungarian girl, Austrian, Swiss and Polish men and of the Germans. Some of them were very nice. What a pity we cannot all live and let live. Perhaps when this is over those of us that are left will be able to be kinder and more understanding than we have been hitherto. I wonder! I am afraid peace settlements will be nearly as bad as the war! All the countries that gave in to Germany without a struggle, as well as those that were overpowered, will all want a say. How glad I am that I am unimportant and will not have to join in the peace struggles!

A certain air raid took place and a man, his wife and mother-in-law or sister-in-law, I don't remember which, went into their reinforced cellar. When 'Raiders Past' signal went his wife said, (as I do) 'well the bombs will begin to drop now. I'm staying here a bit longer.' He said he had to go to work next day so would go to bed. He did. A few minutes later a bomb dropped a direct hit on their house, crashed right through, killing the two women, blowing out the wall of the house, and depositing the man, still in his double bed, clear into the street right side up, too. Wasn't it a wonderful escape for him?

Do you know, you said I might possibly hear from some readers of the Penn Yan paper about my letters. I have never had one single letter! I am really rather sorry as I should have liked to have known what people felt about them

November 8, 1940

Last night the air raid wardens brought our ear plugs. The inhabitants of these Isles have all been issued ear plugs, by a thoughtful government to prevent our ear drums from being smashed during bombardments, or when our own guns fire at the raiders. These plugs are queer little things. I expected something that would look like a wash basin plug! But they are yellowish brown rubber shaped like a woman's 'chubby' umbrella and are mostly too long for ordinary ears, in which case you cut a slight portion off the end, they have to be moistened and then pushed down (or up they said) into the ear as far as they would. How the dickens are we to moisten them if we are out on the street, or most places out of doors! As someone said bluntly – if vulgarly – to me, 'Well lass, you can always use a bit of spit, and after all they're your own ears, so spit won't matter!!' We are to tie them together with eighteen inches of string and attach them to our gas masks. If I ever remember them in case of need I shall feel the age of miracles is not yet over.

I have been enrolled a member of the Women's Voluntary Service corps which means that I along with many other nice women (!) are willing to do any mortal thing that needs to be done in crises and in raids bad, worse or worst. As far as I can see it means doing all the things that nobody else wants to do. The unpaid jobs with no glory attached to them and the necessary assistance behind scenes, such as blankets, hot water for wounds, etc., pails of cold water for fire, bandages, dealing with awkward folk – a specialty of mine! Then my house is to be used as a 'clearing house for the wounded'. I am willing to take anyone in who has been bombed out of their home in this neighbourhood and feed anyone who needs it, help to put out incendiary bombs, in short do anything that has to be done. I am more than willing to do that and more yet, but I do hope that the need for any of it will be unnecessary. So far in this district we have escaped injuries, but that does not mean that we are immune from danger. Just that we have been more than lucky and when we hear bombs dropping in another part of the city we do not know whether it may be our turn to receive the next one that is dropped.

Doris's sister, a nurse in our ████████ was in bed when the first bombs were dropped one night, one on each side of the enormous building and it threw her up out of bed so high she thought she would hit the ceiling, when she came down again she didn't wait for another blast, she got out, seized her clothes and rushed into the ward to see to the patients. The ████████ some of the patients were terribly alarmed. ████████ dropped simultaneously, on each side, so it proves that they were deliberately aiming at the hospital. The kind of thing the Germans habitually do. If there are any decent Germans, how they will loathe their own airmen and how ashamed they will feel. The Germans did bomb a hospital where some of their own men who had been saved were taken. They were furious at being bombed and when a nurse said to them that was what they did to other hospitals now they know what it felt like to be helpless in bed and bombed from above at the same time, they said that their hospital ought to have been left alone. But it wasn't, so I hope some of them learned a useful lesson. But I doubt it.

November 16, 1940

You will have heard about the 'vicious bombing' of Coventry this week. Coventry is one of England's old county towns with a 14th century cathedral, narrow streets and old, old buildings. There is, of course, the newer industrial part as well. But our beautiful cathedral is now in ruins and there are many dead and many terribly injured. But it won't make any difference to the war. We shall still go on.

They bombed Buckingham palace again yesterday. Why, I can't imagine. If they injured or killed our king or queen, it would not stop the war, it would intensify it. For the king and queen are 'one of us', they are our personal friends. They do not have to go about in bullet proof trains, they are not guarded by a detachment of soldiers, the king does not wear armour under his uniform. Neither of them goes about in terror of being shot by some disloyal subject. They are just a man and woman with duties to perform like the rest of us.

The queen has visited hospitals, bombed areas and air raid shelters till I think she must be busy. She speaks to the French soldiers or French air raid casualties in their own language. She talks to the children like any other mother might. She is as distressed as anyone else over the sufferings of air raid victims, asks what she can do to help and does it promptly and efficiently. They both visit factories and talk to the workers, go to the overseas camps and have meals at the canteens and visit the soldiers, ARP posts, fire stations, etc. Everywhere they go they are welcomed and loved the more and always the king puts cheerfulness and heartiness into the men and the queen, with her ready sympathy and understanding mind, encourages everybody to go on bearing everything as cheerfully as possible. She has been very distressed at some of the things she has seen and when Buckingham Palace was bombed the first time, an East-end London woman told her she was so glad that the king and herself were safe. The queen replied 'We are all in this together and we must stand by each other. Is there anything I can do?'

November 20, 1940

About 9:30 p.m. the district superintendent for civil defense had rung me up to discuss matters concerning the effect of poison gas on growing plants, vegetables and crops, etc., when I heard what I thought was some heavy object rolling downstairs. Doris tore along the hall – 'gun firing, guns, Miss Graville.' The DS at the other end of the phone, 'Guns, Miss Graville, I must go.' There had been no warning given or anything but we put out all lights, fetched our gas masks, etc., and prepared for the worst. When Doris and the Dr.

were safely shut up I looked out to see if anything in the immediate neighbourhood was happening. I saw that water was on the boil, made a mental note of what I would use for splints and then sat down to knit and wait. As the gunfire died away we went to bed about 11:15. We had hardly been in bed anytime when we heard the planes. How they missed us I don't know and goodness only knows how many there were. I didn't get up, I was so tired, but never slept a wink. I have another bandaging class this afternoon and a friend for tea so cannot rest.

There is a certain amount of advantage in being awake all night. You have a longer time to think things out and plan accordingly. I thought out what old sheets I could tear up for triangular bandages, what I could use for splints, and arranged how many casualties I could comfortably accommodate in the dining and sitting rooms. The hall I want kept clear to fetch hot water etc. from the kitchen.

I am mean enough to decide to hide my best umbrella, walking stick and sword stick, as those might be appropriated by stretcher parties for splints and there are plenty of other things even unto old newspapers tightly rolled. Oh, how I hope none of it will ever be needed.

The Germans were kind enough to warn us yesterday that 'Coventry was only a flea bite; that much worse was to come.' I'm afraid threats like that leave us unmoved. Good generals do not let their enemies know what they are going to do next. Besides, Hitler couldn't even keep his promise to invade us and be in London by August 15th – and London was ready to receive him too! It still is!

I'm afraid there is no likelihood of my reaching USA before the spring.

November 21, 1940

I received a communication from the home secretary (to whom I wrote in desperation) to say that my application for a passport to

USA is 'being considered'. I applied for permission to sail in the spring. The reason we are stopped sailing is all available ships are needed for necessary war, food, and trade transport and passengers are of small, if any, consideration.

I am not surprised they will not let anyone leave Italy. The British hold command of the Mediterranean and all ships will be stopped and searched, possibly seized, though of course we would never torpedo passenger ships.

Last night we had a most marvelous display of 'fireworks'. I had gone to the front door to look out and to my amazement saw flash after flash of colored lights, then shells bursting, German flares being let down, searchlights in action and yet not a sound of any kind, it was so far away to the south. It was a wonderful exhibition and extraordinary to see without hearing a murmur, but we are very high up, which would, I suppose, explain it. However, it was not many minutes before we heard with a vengeance and more than we liked! The planes sounded so low I felt as if I were outside they would be visible, which I know is not so, but it gives one an awful feeling to hear them so low down and the guns just let bang till the heavens echoed. I am learning to distinguish between gunfire and bombs, though when everything is happening at once it is pandemonium let loose, but it gives me something else to think about, to try to make certain which is which.

I had a letter from a friend in the suburb of a famous northwest city where they have had 259 raids up to now. We can only expect our share. He is in the auxiliary fire service (AFS for short) and said that they had had some thrilling rides and experiences but now they felt the most thrilling thing that could happen to them would be an undisturbed night in bed!

November 22, 1940

Last p.m. the four airmen came. I've never laughed so much for years. I haven't really! One of them had a most infectious laugh and all of them were extremely funny. They were well educated men, quite a different kind from the previous ones. We played Pounce and then Pit. My 'adopted niece' came – she is very attractive and a great asset at these masculine parties!!! So there were six of us. We were in full swing when Doris popped her head round the door – 'Sirens, Miss Graville!' We had never heard a sound, so you can guess the noise we were making. We paused for about two minutes to settle what to do if – and then proceeded with our game. I doubt whether we should have heard gunfire or even bombs! After half an hour 'Raiders past' went, as Doris had to report as we hadn't heard that either! They all came from different parts of the country again. It is very interesting meeting all these different men. One of them remarked on the number of books I had about the Isle of Skye. I was delighted to find that he knew part of the West Highlands where I spent so many happy days in days gone by. I get bits of news that I would love to pass on, but I am learning to keep quiet on such matters! In fact the things 'I don't know' would fill many pages! After the men had gone and I had sobered down, I thought what a dreadful shame and a genuine loss to the country it would be if anything happened to them. For, of course, there are many valuable citizens in our armed forces.

I wish I could give you the rendering of a ridiculous incident that occurred to them and the officer's remarks! It wouldn't be a bit funny if I did – it would lack the wonderful facial expression and tones of voice which made it all the funnier. I have never seen the officer concerned, but I am sure I would know him anywhere! This a.m. I feel as if I had had a tonic. It is nice to see people thoroughly enjoying themselves in one's own house.

Today is one of those wonderful days that makes you forget the war, worry, torrential rains (which are almost habitual now), this morning's air raid, and everything else unpleasant. There isn't a cloud anywhere and the cold wind is as sharp as Sheffield steel. The rosemary on my desk smells delightfully aromatic in the warm room and the sunshine. If I do not look out of the window at the bare trees, I could easily imagine it was a summer's day. The canary has been singing to me and I am just revelling in it. Perhaps tonight we may be lying flat on the floor in the safest part of the house. Let us hope not.

In the intervals of 'war knitting' I am knitting myself a wool frock. I did one two winters ago and nearly lived in it for months. It was the object of envy of friends. I find knitting very soothing to my nerves. I prop a book up in front of me and so do two enjoyable things together, instead of doing one only and wishing all the time I were doing the other. If I am very disgruntled, I find knitting will soon restore me, just as gardening does in suitable weather.

November 23, 1940

We have had three lots of sirens in seven hours beginning at 8:30 p.m. Doris was on her way back from her married sister's. I was what she described as 'all atwitter' until she walked in. Fortunately, the tram stopped near enough for her to walk back by carefully avoiding policemen and air raid wardens making folk take cover! 'I only live five minutes away.' was her plea. I should be very thankful if I could walk that distance in five minutes! Seven league boots would be a necessity for anyone who tried to do it and even then they would be late! A good sound sleep would be a bliss.

It has been arranged that I am to conduct a tour for the four airmen to a place in the country outside Sheffield where there are some very wonderful caves and a famous castle mentioned in one of Sir Walter Scott's novels. The men were very anxious to go, but didn't know how to go, what to see, how to see it, etc., so I diffidently offered my services on the strictest understanding that I pay my own expenses. I refused to go otherwise. They seemed to be frightfully thrilled at the thought of someone who knew it inside out to be willing to take them. I suggested they might like to take some of the Women's Auxiliary Air Force, but they spurned the idea! So it seems I shall have a 'bodyguard' of Royal Air Force men to show the caves, castles, museum, and natural wonders to. I love doing that sort of thing to folk who are genuinely interested in nature. I intend to use such persuasive powers as I possess at the entrances to see if I can get the RAF (being in uniform) in at reduced rates! I didn't know whether it will work, as naturally they get a lot of the military there and the cave owners are rather grasping. They are quite naturally reaping a good harvest while they can.

I suppose this will arrive just before Christmas, so once more a happy time to all of you and great prosperity and good health in 1941.

November 29, 1940

I am still alive, I am thankful to say. Last night our air raid warning sounded at 7:10 p.m. and ended at 4 a.m. – nine hours. When I dropped into bed at 4:30 I was much too awake to sleep. I dare not sleep during the nine hours as I think I told you I have been enrolled as member of the Housewives Service of the Women's Voluntary Service corps. A blue card with a crown on it and 'W.V.S. Housewives Service' printed across is duly fitted in to the top half of the window and informs police, ambulance workers, wardens and all whom it may concern that I have the authority to do certain things in air raids.

I have attended a course of anti-gas and first-aid lectures and feel how terribly incompetent I am, and how mighty little I really know. But at any rate I can allow my house to be a clearing station for the wounded, a refuge for the homeless and I can have hot water, bandages and splints for someone else to use if I do not feel capable. The said card also completely blocks the view of a magnificent hornbeam tree that makes me feel uncomfortable every time I look at it!

After getting everything ready when Wailing Willie howled his warning, I finished some knitting and then read a perfectly lovely book about our country. It was soothing to read about old customs, descriptions of old villages, and tales of bygone farmers and laborers. I don't know how many planes were overhead at that time, but I tried hard to concentrate on a tale about an agricultural show in a remote village and the prize ram getting loose and barging into a farmer's wife who was bending down to pick something up! I know other funny things happened, but I could not pass an examination on the story with any credit! But at least I did at the time know what I was reading about. Fortunately, this neighbourhood escaped, but where the bombs heard were dropped, I do not know. I have not been out today.

I think I mentioned once before that Doris's youngest sister is a nurse in a London hospital. Some foreign refugees were in a shelter quite close to the hospital. When the Germans dropped an aerial torpedo, it went right through the shelter and next a.m. the hospital roof was covered with coats, hats, arms, hands, and legs from the poor victims in the shelter.

November 30, 1940

All round the south and east coasts thousands, yes, literally thousands of dead Germans are being washed up. A man home on leave recently from an important channel port said they were piled up many feet high. It is being a dreadful business for our folk to cope with the burial. It looks as if there had been an attempted invasion, perhaps more than one. I do know that one night some time ago every single man and woman in the country's forces were called out and were on duty. So though we are not told anything, evidently the authorities expected something. Some people near here were fearfully alarmed because soldiers were lining the streets. This is eye witness information and not a wild rumor.

I have been wondering if they knew we were going to get it night before last, as on Wednesday p.m. a pilot officer rang up to say that the men would not be able to come on Thursday. He was sorry he could not give me the reason, but was sure I understood that the war must come first. Their visits will be continued later. So I am in the meantime switching over to the army, as there are some not too far away to get for a jolly time and then when the airmen are at liberty they can come again (and they will lose no time either!) It is nice to know one has given a few of them a pleasant evening when they are so far from their homes. I wish I could do more. I am bound to say I have enjoyed it every bit as much as the men. I have been no martyr over it at all.

The shipping company rang me up yesterday to tell me I'm high up on their list for sailing. I expect I shall be vegetating here by my fireside one week and the next find myself on the high seas with the things I want left at home and surrounded by things I don't want in the least. The shipping company is more than obliging – it's the blessed government so slow in deciding that I can well be spared to leave the country.

During lunch I listened to a broadcast by the (I think) curator of the London zoo, about the animals in war time. All the poisonous snakes were sacrificed at the beginning of the war. Bombs are bad enough without the addition of loose cobras, etc., wriggling about London. The elephants were removed. I have forgotten what happened to the giant cats, tigers and lions, etc. But a bomb dropped outside the zebra house and one zebra got loose. The giraffes were alarmed. One ran round and round the paddock, gave herself heart trouble and died. They thought the antelopes would have panicked and been suffering from broken legs, etc. – next a.m., but they were not in the least perturbed.

The keeper said to him 'You ought to have been here last night, sir. A regular fire works display, it only wanted a band and then you'd have thought it gala night.' That is one of the Londoners whom Hitler and Goering say are sitting cowed, sullen and cringing with fear, in their shelters. It isn't so much fear, as desire for sleep that sends Londoners, below ground at nights. Even the arch liar Goering would be unable to sleep with all the noise going on. Does he lie in bed to seek refuge in an underground shelter when the RAF is over Berlin?

December 4, 1940

I was waked about 1 and 2 a.m. with the most terrific zooming. My room vibrated to it as I've never known it to before. I waited for the inevitable crash, but mercifully the wretched planes passed over. A man was telling me first hand news this a.m. about a bomb nine feet in length weighing 350 cwt (hundred weight – Do you have queer weights as well as queer coinage in the US? – that would be just under 20 tons) that had penetrated 27 feet into the ground. It was a time bomb too, but failed to keep its time! They did not discover its presence for three weeks and that in a busy city! What a mercy it didn't go off, otherwise no one would have known its exact measurements!

December 7, 1940

The men had a jolly time on Thursday p.m. They came from different parts of the country again, one of them from a famous city I love muchly. He told me of the damage that had been done to ancient buildings and priceless possessions till I felt quite murderous. He also described being at the theater during an air raid. The performance was over, a man in the audience had been singing and had just left the stage when three incendiary bombs flopped onto the place where he had been standing. The audience seemed interested to see them put out and anxious to see if any more were dropped! They were in no hurry to leave the building!

I can hardly believe that it is Christmas day a fortnight on Wednesday. Where shall I be the next Christmas day, I wonder? Perhaps somewhere in that mighty country of yours. I wish I could think the world would be at peace. Peace, not an armistice, nor armed non-aggression. But that all countries could have plenty to eat and plenty of things that make peoples prosperous and contented. That when the church bells rang on Christmas day it really meant peace and goodwill. Alas! If British church bells ring at all before the end of the war it means INVASION. (Perhaps by air borne troops). And everyone BEWARE. I thought I heard them the other night and it turned out to be Dr. M's. wireless!!! What a relief!

> **NOTE:** *Sheffield being a major steel and armament manufacturing centre, its residents knew that they would eventually become a major target for the Luftwaffe. Although they had experienced sporadic raids throughout much of 1940, it was nothing compared to what happened the night of 12–13 December 1940. The first warning sirens went off around 7 p.m. and the all clear didn't sound until after 4 a.m. Around 280 German aircraft dropped over 10,000 bombs of various types. The results were devastating – over 600 civilian deaths, 1,500 wounded, 3,000 homes and shops damaged beyond repair, a total of 82,000 properties damaged and one tenth of the population of the city left homeless. It became known in Britain as the Sheffield Blitz.*

December 13, 1940

How is it that I am alive, I cannot understand. Last night we had nine hours continuous bombing at the rate of three a minute. It was terrible. Never shall I forget it. Today I had to go into the city and the scenes I saw were appalling. The bombing was nothing but sheer wanton destruction. No military objectives whatever, simply residential and business districts. The city was a raging inferno at 5 a.m. I slipped out to a vantage point a couple of minutes away. It was a marvelous spectacle, but dreadfully tragic. We dropped into bed at 5:30 a.m. It had been a night of almost unearthly brilliancy, the moonlight was startling clear. So there was no excuse for the indiscriminate bombing.

When two awful explosions occurred close together, the house rocked, tilted, stayed poised for what seemed ages, though probably was only for a second. I looked at the ceiling and wondered whether the pendant electric lights would strike me. There wasn't time for us to lie flat. Fortunately the house righted itself. It almost seemed as if the house paused to think. It was a breathtaking moment.

I had four soldiers from one of the barracks and they stayed with us till 11:30 as shrapnel and bombs were raining down and as they ought to have been in at 10 p.m. promptly, they dared not stay any longer. They thought they would be needed for rescue and demolition work. Every policeman, fireman, special constable, auxiliary fireman, air raid warden, woman ambulance driver, first aid workers, etc., in the city were at it and have been all day. Bus loads of policemen, etc., came from other places to help. Many delayed action bombs have been dropped and whole streets are roped off. Thousands are without water, gas or electricity. Fortunately we have water, the electricity was only off for about an hour, but the gas went off when a gasometer blew up nearly five miles away. I thought every window was gone then. The guns nearly finished my windows too. But I've come to the conclusion that the fact all the windows and doors fit so badly was an asset then, as it gave them play. The front door nearly blew in and when one of the men had gone upstairs he came tearing down after a much too near bomb had dropped and said the landing walls literally caved in. They dropped hundreds of incendiary bombs all round us, but mercifully not on us. It got to be quite a game of skill to tell which was bomb and which was gun when they were nearly simultaneous.

While the men were here we played rummy and Slippery Ann, (NOTE: card game also known as Hearts) with the men telling us what sort of planes were overhead. I was not interested in the kind of plane but only the position! There must have been hundreds of them. They dropped some of the evil land mines which made craters thirty feet deep and more across and buried houses by the score.

No shops were open in the city especially, no transport could run, we had no newspapers or anything. I saw fire engines and ambulances overturned into craters, or burnt out. One of our largest hospitals is being evacuated on account of the bombing it received. Our beautiful city hall with its famous vestibule has no windows, the wonderful vestibule is a mass of wreckage and the wrought iron gates, considered beautiful by those who like such things, damaged, the pillars chipped and the steps ruined.

What good to the war effort has any of that done? I saw people pathetically searching among the safer ruins for their possessions, others with tragically small bundles, representing their all, and people with bandages, weary faces and tired bodies, but not one ever suggested we should sue for peace. I spoke to several unfortunates and there was never a word of complaint, only sympathy for others. One man said, 'Eh, but our chaps will give them hell for this.' A woman standing outside the shell of what was once her home said, 'When this happened' – with a wave of a grimy hand, 'I told myself our boys would be giving them worse in Germany, so we can stand it all right.' Two of our most famous shops are burnt out completely. The broken glass was being shoveled up into enormous lorries, like the snow being removed. The streets everywhere were literally paved with broken glass; snow and slush lying in the gutters and where it was not slippery mud, there were sheets of glass where the water had frozen when poured on to the burning houses. The firemen have been amazingly good at getting the fires under control. Many buildings are still smouldering. I hope no wind comes up or it will be as bad as bombs again.

A deacon of my church and his wife have been burnt to death in their reinforced cellar and a Methodist minister's wife, about 15 minutes walk from here, is believed to be buried under the ruins of her house. Her daughter-in-law told me this afternoon, someone said he saw her taken out and sent to a hospital. They've been to every hospital in Sheffield and cannot find any trace of her. The soldiers who are trying to get at her say she is there and must be dead. Isn't it dreadful? Those are only two cases, but when you think of them being multiplied many times it makes you feel, very, very sad.

A delayed action bomb fell about two minutes walk away. We were told to expect it to go off this afternoon and I wondered if I should get home to find all the windows gone. But it is delaying its action, to keep us guessing, I suppose! I think I walked about eight miles this afternoon with ruination and damage on all sides. I don't see how they can get glass renewed at present in the huge quantities that are – and will be – needed.

December 14, 1940

We went to bed at nine. So, after two nights out of bed it was delightful to have a quiet night.

I am very anxious about friends and the telephones are all out of order, so cannot contact them. It is awfully cold and as my house is heated throughout with gas fires, except the kitchen, we have no heat and do not know when we shall get any. By the looks of things yesterday, not yet awhile. But I have a roof over my head and some food and my life with an uninjured body, so there: nothing to grumble about and much to be thankful for. Thousands of people are homeless, many more with no windows, no water, no gas and no electricity and partially damaged houses.

We actually have a newspaper today and the German radio says that they gave us a similar raid in Coventry. I can assure you that for the first time since the war they spoke the truth!! Though they have made a good many misstatements, one of them being the parts of the city, their compasses must even lie, like the makers. Several cinemas and a music hall with audiences were wrecked. Schools, except for evening classes, would be empty and they have been badly hit.

I have been gathering a big parcel of clothing this a.m. Doris has given me some warm woolly jumpers, etc. With my knitted wool frock and a variety of other things, there are enough garments of one sort or another to help to clothe one or two women. Doris is going to walk to the city (three miles each way) and it is driving rain with a southeast bitter wind to take them to the town hall for distribution. Oh, at times like this you feel shortage of money so keenly. Wouldn't it be lovely to be able to go into a shop and buy a dozen good blankets and warm clothes and say 'here you are' to some of those brave suffering souls?

On the whole, I am glad to see the rain (though it certainly does not warm us!) as it will help to put out the still burning fires and perhaps prevent fires breaking out again, though it will add to the difficulties of the clearing squads. Those qualified to say, think there were anywhere from 200 to 500 planes over us. Our gunners brought down two, which was very wonderful as the planes were a terrific height up in the ballooned areas. I imagine one of the extraordinary noises (among many) that we heard must have been the plane exploding. But things were exploding all night.

An ambulance left one of the first aid posts and has never been seen since. I saw a horrid mess on the pavement and an ambulance worker said 'that is all that is left of two soldiers'. Some of the men at the barracks, where my Thursday evening men are stationed, were killed on the premises and ever so many were deliberately bombed whilst on rescue work, a number were blown up when a gasometer was bombed while they were trying to get people away to safety. I have wondered so often if any of the men who have been here were among them. They were such nice fellows.

An errand girl has just been here. She lives near our biggest hospital, and says they must have been aiming at it for all around is a dreadful mess. They have no gas, water, electricity or windows and many round them are buried, killed or maimed. I don't want you to think I'm whining please, but I am sure a detailed, first hand, true, unexaggerated account will interest you and be good for those Americans who think America should stand aloof. The night of the raid I was amazed to find my chief feeling was that of rage rather than fear. And after my explorations yesterday my blood boiled when I saw the bombed hospital and saw them carrying out victims who would have to be removed elsewhere, poor souls, when all they wanted was comfort and peace where they could get well again.

All our buses were used for ambulances as they bombed any ambulance they could. When the men were here we heard machine gunning outside the ballooned area. They came down lower and attacked those who were helping with fire and the wounded. The brilliant moonlight would have allowed them to see a beetle crawling on the road, to say nothing of the glare from the huge fires. I think it is nothing short of a miracle that the whole fourteen miles of the city area was not burnt out.

I saw some of the fire fighters yesterday. They were unrecognizable through dirt, their eyes were blood shot, they looked as if they were too tired to lift their feet off the ground, yet when they were able to leave a building with safety all they said was 'Well now, what about so and so,' naming some other burning building and away they went with their hose and special engine and a smile for the bystanders. 'That'll give no more trouble lady,' one said to me as he left an odd wall or two of what a few hours before had been an old established shop on one of the main streets.

During the raid I had to keep running upstairs when I heard noises that I couldn't recognize to see if incendiary bombs had come through the roof.

I met a first aid woman over 60 years old who lives near me. She had been on duty at one of the railway stations. When asked about her rheumatism she said, 'Rheumatism! Rheumatism! My dear woman I spent the night lying flat and getting up again, in between bandaging the soldiers. Don't talk to me about rheumatism!!'

After all this you will realize that at the moment I am still alive. But if anything worse comes I do not see how I could escape then. Don't worry if you don't hear, it's the good who die young and I cannot claim first youth. We are still unbeaten though a bit bombed and inconvenienced, but we are learning what a lot of splendid people there are in the world. We are going to win, so that's all there is to be said.

> **NOTE:** *Sheffield suffered a second massive attack on 15 December 1940. Nearly a hundred bombers dropped a large number of incendiary bombs over the course of three hours, leaving the city ablaze. The steel works were the major targets, although the city centre experienced most of the damage.*

January 1, 1941

We have started the new year well. Yesterday afternoon sleet began to fall and this a.m. we woke to a white world. As I look out of the window, every twig and branch of the trees is outlined in white. It is very beautiful to look at, but very cold and slippery outside.

I expect you have received my letter telling you about our two dreadful air raids. I have had no time to write letters. I did not even get some of my Christmas presents off until a couple of days ago. Everyone who was intact had to set to and see to the 80,000 homeless and all the thousands whose houses were partially damaged, or who had to be temporarily evacuated on account of time bombs. There were thousands without water. No one in Sheffield has any gas and we may not have it for a long time. Those of us who had clothes had to turn out as many as possible for those who had only what they stood up in. A friend of mine who had the most expensive clothes of anyone I know, with furniture to match (her bed was an old one and valued at 100 pounds) had an incendiary bomb in her flat and she was more than grateful to accept an old coat of mine – six years old!

The day after our first terrible ordeal, as I went about among the ruins, I felt the world was full of hate and evil, but I soon began to realize what a host of kind-hearted people there were. Everyone was so anxious to do all they could for others less fortunate than themselves. And when I heard of the many acts of heroism performed by people you would never think could do anything at all, I just felt humbled beyond measure to have escaped so lightly and without effort.

On Christmas day I had four soldiers for the afternoon and evening. One of them arrived at two o'clock. I had just come downstairs from a bath and changing and had promised myself half an hour's sit with a book, not having had any time since the blitz to indulge thus. So I had to begin straight away. On boxing night I had offered to take six and one brought a pal, so there were seven. We had a most hilarious evening. I wished I were a millionaire living in a baronial hall, for the men had two whole days off till midnight each day and literally nowhere to go as all the places of amusement and halls especially arranged for their comfort were either burnt out or else flat. They had a very dull time. So many people had lost their homes or were full to bursting point with evacuees themselves, they had no room for entertaining soldiers or anyone else.

Today I am expecting four more and only hope they will enjoy themselves as much as the others did. One of the men was a born comic and kept us all in fits of laughter all evening. He had only to begin to laugh to set the rest of us going. What a godsend a man like him must be in the army. On boxing day some of them belonged to the Bomb Disposal Squad. They told me some appalling facts about their rescue work from one of the hospitals. I would not let them talk about it much as one of them said he only wished he could forget some of the sights he had witnessed, but he said they were before his eyes the whole time. He spoke of the plucky nurses and the women in the maternity ward, one of whom was in agony in the labor ward when the place was hit and had to be carefully moved to safety. The others seemed to think that putting a time bomb out of action was a joke. When I shuddered, he said: 'But think what a sell for old Hitler every time one of his bombs is spoilt. Think of all the people who aren't killed.' No thought of their own danger; all of it taken as a matter of course.

January 3, 1941

I am going out to lunch with a friend today. She is the kind who makes up a huge fire, puts the most comfy chair close to it with me inside it, and then proceeds to give me the kinds of things to eat she knows I like and which are difficult to get. We always have a good laugh over our problems and I tease her husband about his air raid warden's duties. They think I'm quite daft to go to the US. I have managed to persuade them that Americans are a civilized people and that I do not anticipate being murdered in my bed, knifed in the street, or poisoned at dinner!

We still have no gas nearly a month after the Blitz. It is simply wonderful the way in which the services have got going again so quickly. I think most people have water again and many houses have managed to have their windows boarded up, if not glass put in, and temporary roofs fitted. The transport has started again, too. We have had several warnings, but thank goodness, no further bombings, though we hear of other places in trouble.

On New Year's night, I had four soldiers for the evening. A warning sounded before they came and I thought they would not come, but they did. They said they were not going to turn back! Raiders Past sounded soon after, but about 10 o'clock another warning sounded, so we learnt afterwards!!! But we were making such a row playing Pit, that we didn't hear it and Doris, to her astonishment, snugly in bed at 2 a.m., heard Raiders Past sounded! I feel very guilty for of course I too was in bed and I am supposed to be ready with hot water, splints and bandages etc. Fortunately, nothing happened, though we should have heard gunfire. I wonder when the men found out. They were lance corporals and should have been ready too! They had a late pass and would not get back until midnight. I'm expecting them again next week. They were such very nice men that I asked them again. Usually different ones come each week and I do not see them again except when they drive past the house. They had been engaged in rescue work and some of their experiences were gruesome and ghastly beyond description. The tortures of the damned in Dante's Inferno were a picnic compared to the sufferings of some of the victims in the raids.

January 5, 1941

I have spent most of the a.m. trying to thaw the outlet pipe from the scullery sink, a very unsabbatical operation but it had no business to be frozen. I am always very careful about the outlets and am very cross about it. But anger did not thaw it – red hot pokers, boiling water, and an electric radiator helped.

We had two warnings during the night. A few folk will suffer from chills getting up out of warm beds and padding over snow and ice to sit in chilly shelters till such time as the powers that be ordain that they may emerge to light and home again.

Once more, please let America know that, though we are rationed, we are not starving. Though we are bombed, we are not beaten and though Americans are fond of saying 'the British have their backs to the wall' we have our faces and guns to the enemy.

January 15, 1941

Sheffield is rising nobly from the ashes (literally) of the blitz. Such shops as are left are all boarded up and bear notices like 'Open – more than usual' (!) 'Blitz & Blast – still open', 'Hitler tried to close us, but we are still open'; 'Hitler was our last customer; will you be our next?' etc.

In the miles of ruins of nothing but twisted girders and heaps of bricks (some of which, by the way, are still smouldering) notices are stuck up: 'Messers. Blank, Temporary Premises.' Then follows the address of a building they have found somewhere where they can carry on. For carry on we all do. I am thrilled to the marrow (though I'm not quite sure if I have any marrow) at the way everyone has set to and got going again. We just keep on keeping on, and everyone helps where one can. The folk who have been affected the most and who have lost everything they possess, sometimes relatives included, are absolutely fine. Not a word of grumbling. When some who lost their all asked me 'How did you go on?' I feel almost ashamed to be safe with a roof over my head, although I'd no heating! I had at least a house and water.

I was looking at some of my old treasures, the other day, and imagined what I should feel like if some of my 16th century possessions had gone forever. A friend of mine in a small Yorkshire town has a house full of evacuees, and said in a letter to me the other day, that the house was so full of people, she had no room for her treasures and was trying to make herself part with them (it is difficult to get rid of things that are really good, or useful) and she ended by saying, 'Perhaps it will suddenly be done for me!' They had a bomb very near their house!

I must confess I grieve when some of England's priceless old buildings and possessions vanish in a second through senseless wanton destruction. The Sheffield blitzes were nothing short of mass murder.

Last week, I sent you H. V. Morton's 'London'. He has written some delightful books about this country which, now that the

Germans are destroying so much that was lovely, will be valuable history as well as pleasant reading in the future.

January 16, 1941

To be fetched out of bed at 4 a.m. by the sounds of bombs and of planes so low you feel they may hit the chimneys is not a pleasant way of beginning the day. But it is all part of our lives. There was a warning at 9:20 p.m. till 1 a.m. So I was very cross with the Germans disturbing me at 4 a.m. out of a sleep provided by the doctor via a pill of some sort. I have been under him for insomnia again and to be waked violently makes me feel very rotten. However, I'm still alive!

I have now got two women students from the university, as their hall (of residence) has no gas and they cannot cook for the students. We are having terribly cold frosty weather. The buckets of water placed outside each house to assist the fire parties put out fires caused by incendiary bombs are all frozen solid. The reason that fires did so much damage during the two blitzes was that water mains were hit and volume of water poured out where no water was required and whole districts had none at all. Some people have never been found at all just burnt to ashes or blown to bits.

A working woman of the size of an anti-aircraft balloon (or thereabouts) said to me the day before yesterday, 'Lord Haw Haw says that 'Itler is coming tonight, but I'm losing no sleep over 'im; I get all the sleep I can and then when he does come, I'm ready. 'Itler, who's he I'd like to know? I'm not worrying we've got our lads and Mr. Churchill; 'Itler'll soon know it.' I wish all American and European neutrals could have heard the scorn in her voice when she asked, ''Itler, who's he, I'd like to know?' I think the bombastic little upstart would have collapsed himself even if he could have heard her, and remember she expresses the views of the British nation. Though

I think of the two, Mussolini is held to be the most contemptible and Hitler, the most evil.

I wonder if the men will turn up tonight. Last week, the sirens prevented the ones who were expecting to come, as their particular duties demand they should stand by whenever Willie wails and he wailed all night – a seven hour 'do'.

Perhaps you are puzzled because I mention the two blitzes and no other raids. That is because the others are raids and those two nights were simply and solely mass murder and wanton destruction carried out by relays of planes any number up to 500 altogether. I could tell you a great deal, but I do not want to get on the wrong side of the censor. My lifelong regret will be that I was not among those who saw the last of the five shot down on the second occasion. ARP wardens, fire watchers, police, etc., saw a marvelous spectacle of one shot literally to pieces, complete with its loads of bombs several thousands of feet up. They say the firework display was unbelievable and pieces of the plane were picked up very far apart. I had been watching bursting shells and tracer bullets, etc, from an upstairs window (contrary to regulations!) where I had gone to see if much of the city was again on fire. I dare not go out, as I do not yet possess a 'tin hat'. Oh! I've just remembered I have a German helmet which a friend brought me back from the last war. I don't think I turned it out when they called for 'scrap' metal. What better purpose for a German helmet than to protect the head of a loyal Englishwoman? That is if my head will not crack under its weight, which is terrific. I must look for it.

They wanted me to join the 'fire watchers', but I can't be indoors attending to the afflicted and out-of-doors putting out incendiary bombs. But I shall do that in between times, no doubt. I shall treat someone for shock, and then say to them very solemnly, 'Now, lie quite still; you'll be all right here' and then run out and throw a bucket of sand on an incendiary and then run in and administer hot very sweet drinks to the patients. At least that is what I should do; I only hope I shall not throw a bucket of sand over the 'shock' cases and the sweet drinks over the incendiary bomb!

January 19, 1941

To add to our plentiful difficulties, we have had a terrific snowstorm and we had to dig ourselves out of the house this morning. The two students cleared the path for me so I only had to move the drift outside the back door and they did the rest.

Yesterday afternoon I attended the ceremony of the opening of a headquarters room for the wardens who are mostly men. It was to be opened by the Lord Mayor, the lady mayoress came too. Probably the fact that I can come to the US helped, but I haven't enjoyed any public functions so much for many moons. It was entirely for the air raid wardens, police officials, and fire watchers, but as a special favor four of the WVSHS were invited and I was one of them. The Lord Mayor was late, so one of the city ARP officials tried to accompany us on the piano (without music) for community singing and didn't I sing!!

By the time the chairman had finished inviting 'old friends' to say a few words – which by the way were not always few – the meeting lasted an hour and a quarter later than it should have done. But it was all very jolly and friendly. At the close I was bolting for the door when I was called back to be presented (with the other three ladies) to the lord mayor and lady mayoress. As I have known the latter for some years, it was rather fun.

The chief warden was awarded a very high honor by the king, when he and the queen were in Sheffield last week, for his very daring work on the nights of the blitzes and for his brilliant leadership of the wardens in the whole city since war began.

One or two of the speakers told us some funny stories of things that happened on the nights of the blitzes. It was all so terrible that I feel that I don't want to laugh about anything and yet even in the middle of that mass murder there were humorous incidents, though admittedly they were few. Poor old Sheffield. How they bombed us and what wonderful deeds of daring were performed by so many who will ever be unsung, for everyone was so busy doing what they could that there was no time to watch other people.

The lord mayor told us of some young girls (I believe they were girl guides, but am not certain) who went on messenger duty at 4 p.m. on the day of the first blitz; as the relief messengers could not get through they stuck to their posts through the bombing till 11 p.m. next night (Friday) without any food or cups of tea – merely drinks of water. Quite a number of boys all over the country have been wonderfully quick in getting fires under control before the fire services could reach them.

You will notice that though I have not done anything brave myself, I am so proud of our boys and girls that have and of all the men and women who have done so much to help. It seems that Hitler's new move is to burn us out. They've got a new kind of bomb that scatters a sort of fire very difficult to extinguish to loose on us now. I am very distressed to think of all the priceless buildings and treasures being destroyed forever. Although these things were British, I regard them as belonging, in a sense, to all thinking beauty loving men and women the world over. I feel positively murderous when I hear of this and that being irrevocably destroyed, for some things can never be replaced or rebuilt and the world will suffer as a result.

January 20, 1941

We have had a fearful snowstorm. Of course, no mention in the papers, but traffic is seriously affected. I went down into the city this afternoon. It was terrible getting about, and so pathetic to see old, really old, men shoveling snow into the clearance lorries, all the young men being at the war. The bombed ruins of once fine shops looked very desolate with several feet of snow over the piles of bricks and twisted girders. One shop has been smoldering ever since and today broke into fire again although it seemed nothing but a heap of bricks. I watched the firemen emptying gallons of water into the heap and was interested to note that what I had taken to be a leak in the pipe which (quite unnecessarily) sprayed me all over as I passed hurriedly to try to get a tram home, was in reality a fine spray soaking onto surrounding buildings, or shells of building nearby in order to prevent them from being set alight by sparks. How anything can catch fire in this dreadful snowstorm I don't know – icicles many feet long hanging from what was once the beauty parlor of one of our biggest shops and snow many feet deep everywhere.

NOTE: *Along with the letter in the* Chronicle-Express *of 27 February 1941 was this:*

Miss Graville, who is completing arrangements to come to this country in the spring for a visit and lecture tour, enclosed with this letter a clipping from the Sheffield Telegraph and Independent of January 20 telling of a citizen of Ireland who happened to be in the city the night of the first blitz and was so impressed by the bravery of the people that he sent the Prime Minister a note for one pound to help with the relief work. To quote a paragraph from his letter: 'All my life until that night I thought we Irish were a long-suffering brave race, but after ten minutes of a nine-hour German murderous bombardment of your women and children, my childhood teaching left me cold, because never in world history could such bravery be displayed as I witnessed among your people that night.'

January 28, 1941

I have received some delightfully kind letters from several readers of my letters in the *Chronicle-Express* and I do appreciate them very much. To come down in the morning (American mail usually arrives in the a.m.) after a night disturbed by air raids or worries caused by war and to find a letter from someone on the other side of the world where life goes on normally, free of air raids, rationing, blackouts, dislocated transport, and above all free from WAR, gives one a nice warm glow all over. It is nice to know that over there where life goes on normally, unknown friends are interested enough to write. This friendliness is indeed heartening and cheering. Several letters arrived yesterday and this morning's post brought me four more. I am replying to all personally and I wish they knew how much pleasure their kind letters are giving me. I am due at WVS meeting tomorrow and am going to read some of these messages of goodwill which I have received from America.

January 29, 1941

Everyone who writes to me from the US – or nearly everyone – mentions the beauty and peacefulness of the English countryside. It is that peacefulness that we British love, and one of the things for which we are fighting. It is not only in the beautiful countryside that we have peacefulness that is part of our land, but here only a few minutes walk away, you can wander through a beautiful, peaceful wood – within the city boundaries, too. The only sounds to be heard are the rilling of the streams, the call of the woodpeckers, the chattering of squirrels, the songs of the birds, and the rustling of leaves in the breeze.

In spring these woods are carpeted with bluebells, acres of misty blue, with a delicate perfume, enhanced by a warm shower, all the trees assuming a fairy-like mantle of soft green – of many, many shades, all blending one with another with an effect no human being can ever achieve, however artistic.

In autumn these same woods glow with the glory of brilliant colors, with the rays of the setting sun shining on to them, the trees whose green entranced us so early in the year, now leave us breathless with wonder that they are so lovely. We see it year after year and yet it always seems lovelier than ever before! I always feel the trees are glowing with pride at the fall of the year, for all the glory and joy they have given us and the use they have been to the birds, insects, and animals inhabiting the woods, as if saying goodbye to us and blushing while they tell us they will be beautiful again in a few months time after a little while for a rest and recuperation. To me, trees are every bit as lovely in their winter forms as when in tender budding leaf. I long for a really good photograph of bare branches against a winter sunset for my 'Folklore of Trees' lecture.

The road is in an appalling state and a lorry has got stuck bang in the middle. All other vehicles are held up owing to the high banks of snow cleared from the center.

I can hear what sounds like a plane. Doris has gone to see her married sister just over the city boundary miles away on the other side. It is a strange thing, but practically every time she decides to visit her sister, the Nazis decide to visit us! So far, she has managed to get back, but I do not want her stuck for hours in a shelter in the middle of the city, should she be unlucky enough to get caught too far away to get back within a few minutes of the sirens' warning. But, of course, we cannot stop indoors forever for fear of warnings!

I still have four soldiers on Thursday evenings, and have been making mince pies for them tomorrow night and Yorkshire parkies. When I can give them home-made fare, it does vanish quickly!

February 1, 1941

Today is bright sunshine and blue sky, to be followed tonight in all probability by air raids. It is lovely to see the sunshine after a fortnight of fog, and we live for the moment only in these days, and are enjoying the sun, sky, and trees, etc.

February 2, 1941

By tradition, snowdrops ought to be out today in their thousands, as it is the 'Fair Maids of February' are hidden under a thick blanket of snow. It is a perfect morning, blue sky, bright sunshine, and keen frost; the tracery of the trees against the sky is a glorious study of blue-black. The temptation to gaze out of the window instead of getting on with a pile of letters is a menacing one! Surely it never does us any harm to drink in all the beauty we can. The magpies have begun to rest, and there is a very old superstition about what is to happen when they do that. I must look it up and then tell you sometime.

I have been looking at my rose trees. Already the one climbing up the house by the front door is showing signs of bud to the initiated. I wonder if I shall see it again. By the way, talking of roses, do you know that my grandmother (and your great-aunt, being one and the same woman) followed the old English custom of putting dark red fragrant rose petals under the pastry in a cherry pie. Oh, if only I could eat one of her cherry pies now. Though I was only about ten years old or so when she died, I remember those pies very well. I have always been very fond of cherry pie, but somehow they never seem to taste as good as hers did. Quite undeservedly I was her favorite grandchild. I did not see her nearly as often as I would have liked. My father insisted that she spoilt me, and he would not allow it. I never believed – in those days at any rate! – that she did. It would be lovely to be 'spoilt' again. But when grown up, one never is, unfortunately.

February 5, 1941

We are having a most awful blizzard at the moment. At any rate, we can't have an air raid! But it is a terrible night. The snow is drifting while you wait, and nearly blinds you; the wind is like sharp steel. What we shall find in the morning goodness only knows. It is even drifting through cracks in the window panes, under doors, through the letter box, etc. I have electric radiators on in the scullery, 'House of Commons', and hall, to keep pipes from freezing. The bathroom is warmed by the hot water cistern, and of course the kitchen will be kept warm by the fire. But we are so tired of snow and ice. I am sorry for the people whose windows were blown out or smashed during the blitzes, for in many cases they have been temporarily repaired with some patent material, supposed to be weather-proof, but certainly not glass.

I was very disappointed along with everyone else that Wendell Willkie had to leave England without visiting Sheffield. A letter from the lord mayor's secretary to say that Mr. W. would not be coming arrived this a.m. after I had heard in last night's news that he was returning to US at once.

February 6, 1941

After the blizzard and a sudden thaw, road conditions are too awful to describe. I ought to have gone into the city, but dare not risk it with my 'gamey' foot, so have sent Doris instead. Which reminds me of the story of a woman who objected to her daughter's going out to post an important letter on a very wild night, said the woman emphatically, 'It's not fit to turn a dog out, we'll send father!'

I got up to begin sorting when my attention was attracted by a jug of Chinese lanterns, which before Christmas I wired onto long sprays of Berberis Sterophylea (originally raised in Sheffield). To my surprise and delight, the sprays are starred with budding flowers. It will be an unusual sight when they come out – if they do – to have Chinese lanterns and Berberis flowers growing (apparently) on one stem! I must cherish them and photograph them.

Then the telephone went, and I had a prolonged conversation with Mr. C. who told me of the death of a mutual acquaintance, caused by a bomb in a raid the other night. He is a special constable and had to go on duty and was present when the rescue party brought out the man concerned.

Tonight should be soldiers' night. But if enemy planes are about, some of them have to stand by, so I never know whether they are coming till they arrive, and it looks as if it would be an ideal raid night.

Doris has told me of a yellow crocus under the sitting room window. The snow is thawing rapidly, and I found the first snowdrop. The daffodils are romping up, but I don't expect to see them in flower, the grape hyacinths are having a race with the scillas, but I don't expect to see them either. But, it is lovely to see everything shooting up, it means the turn of the year, and that spring is on its way.

NOTE: *This followed the letter above in the 13 March 1941 issue of the* Chronicle-Express:

Mrs. Anne Wood, 16 Maiden lane, Penn Yan, has received an interesting letter from Miss Graville, Sheffield, England, telling about the December air raids which were described in her recent letters appearing in the *Chronicle-Express*. Mrs. Wood has a brother living at 12 Lincoln Crescent, St. Helens, Lancaster, England, who in a recent letter said: 'Just had an air raid warning, but it didn't last long. Suppose you know we all have air raid shelters in the back garden, although some are built in the streets. Everyone carries his gas mask wherever he goes. Every town has firemen, stationed at different points, ready to tackle the fires. It is a general thing for the Germans to drop fire bombs, and then, when the fires get going, to follow up with the bombing. We have guns around here that shake the house, and some nights are like the 5th of November, the sky being lit with searchlights and shells. One bomb dropped in the garden opposite us. We heard it coming, but it didn't go off. It sure gives you a nasty feeling. It's surprising, but the kids take it all better than we, but it's doing them no good stopping up at night.'

February 13, 1941

At last, I have news that I may be able to sail for America this spring. I will not know the name of the boat until I am on it, and I will not be allowed to write the date of the sailing. Of course, I may be delayed even then – had no idea there were so many forms to be filled out. I have had my passport photos (nine of them) taken here in the city, but I have to go to Manchester to have my visas stamped as the United States consul has left Sheffield. He found it a bit too warm, I fancy.

My bank manager has advised me to sell every stick of furniture lest it go up in smoke during my absence. I am going to loan my old Georgian dining table to my doctor for the time I am away for his wife admires it so much. They are also going to store some valuable pictures for me. I am giving his little boy a portable writing desk made by hand by one of the last people in England to make furniture entirely by hand. So many people have lost stored furniture through enemy action.

I wish someone would send me a list of things which could be brought into the United States duty free. Any travel advice pertaining to the United States will also be thankfully received.

The Civil Defense service is expecting me to give a number of lectures on 'Herbs in War Time'. I don't know if I shall be able to now. I may also have to cancel a lecture in Derby.

The manager of the Cunard line suggests you leave a letter of instructions with the New York office to be delivered to me when the boat docks.

February 26, 1941

Your letter posted January 6 arrived February 21. J. H. happened to be here when it arrived and said to tell you that there is a new admiralty order that Royal Navy men cannot receive letters direct from foreign countries, only newspapers and magazines; letters must be sent to their homes first.

You ask if I would like you to send me any food. Our supplies are ample and the butter ration is to be raised shortly. I am wondering if any of your readers would like to send spare babies' and children's clothes for some of the bombed out families of Sheffield. If so they would be doing a real service. They are badly needed at the Women's Voluntary Service Depot, Sheffield, England.

If they mention whom they are from, they might like to say they are in response to my appeal as my name is known to the WVS. Anything that is clean, mended and wearable for the innocent little victims of these terrible raids will be greatly appreciated. When I come I shall be able to give you an idea of how badly these things are needed and to thank you on behalf of the sufferers of Nazi brutality.

I have a contract with the editor of the Sheffield evening paper for a weekly news letter from the USA for the two years I expect to be there. He will not be allowed to send money out of the country in payment so is going to pay it direct to my bank here.

I am reading all the books by Americans that I can. Have just finished 'Through China's Wall' by Graham Peck. How I've enjoyed it, and recommended it to friends. My library subscription runs out in March, but I shall not renew it as I am so uncertain of the time I shall be here.

I am hoping to do some radio broadcasting in America. Tomorrow afternoon I have to speak to a WVS gathering.

I am bringing Barbara a jumper knitted by the Shetland knitters in the Fair Isle pattern. The wools are all home dyed by the knitters themselves. The wool is from their own sheep and is spun by their own hands (the knitters' not the sheep). I can order things from these knitters while I am in USA. I should be pleased to help them as their work is beautiful, and the shops pay them so little. I wish their work were better known. It is so lovely, and the Shetlanders have a hard life. My favorite meal, tea, is now ready.

March 1, 1941

My passport has arrived! I am now waiting for a passage, but as I already explained I cannot let you know when I am leaving; can send only a guarded cable.

Yesterday I talked to a nurse who has been in London for about eighteen months. I asked her about the London people, if they were scared, or worn out, or queuing up for food. She replied that from their demeanor one would never know that there was a war at all. There is no food shortage, and theaters, shops, cinemas, and music halls are open as usual. Everyone goes into shelters to sleep. Anyone who suggested giving in would be nearly lynched. She has been in the very thick of things and she is the nurse who helped the doctor whom the king recently decorated for bravery. She was with him in rescue work the night he refused to seek safety and worked to save victims until his back was broken. He is now in a cast but carrying on with his work as much as possible. I feel proud to be of the same nationality as such brave people.

I find I have to pay two pounds capitation tax to enter the United States. It sounds rather suggestive as though I were to be hanged and charged for it. Several people have made appointments through my solicitor to view the house. It is to be sold Tuesday. The snow drops are out, so are the yellow crocuses and two Winter aeomites. The lilac buds are fat and the leaves of the golden elder are actually showing color. I went out to make a farewell inspection of the garden this morning. The snow has gone and many plants are already up. I was surprised to see them. They really seemed to say, 'We thought we'd like to see you again before you went. Please don't leave us to someone who won't look after us or love us as you have.' I feel as though I were deserting them. It is the garden I shall miss most when I am in the States.

When I started packing I wondered how I should fill my trunks. Now I am wondering how I shall shut them.

NOTE: *Winifred M. Graville sold her home on Ringinglow Road in March 1941. She anticipated a two-year lecture tour of the United States, hoping that the lectures and her writing would sustain her financially. As indicated in her letters, she was having quite a bit of trouble getting out of England during wartime. While waiting, she lived with friends in different parts of Sheffield.*

April 3, 1941

26 Chatsworth Road, Totley Rise, Sheffield, Eng.

I came here on Monday, leaving the old home for good and all. My friend, with whom I am staying, is kindness itself. She has a beautiful home full of lovely old furniture, old china and silver. Her husband is in charge of the electric plant of Sheffield and the house is full of every conceivable electric gadget that is conducive towards comfort and efficiency.

As I lie in bed in the mornings, I look out to the huge rampart of moorland and when the wind is in the right direction we can smell the moors. A lovely scent, that of wet moorland, quite indescribable but it brings to all moorland lovers a mental vision of big shoulders of land covered in winter with heavy shades of soft browns and gray greens; in spring with bright tips to the heather plants; in summer tracts of colored grasses, with pools of peat water shining bright blue under a summer sky or a blackish brown under rain clouds, and in another direction the bright reddish purple stretching for miles, away to the horizon with the exquisite scent of the heather – it is a treasured vision. And the sound of the grouse calling, 'Go back, go back,' to all who live near the moors is loved music. I am glad that I have lived so close to our wonderful moorlands. There is something so bracing to the mind as well as body, to stand there with great stretches of moorland about, and a silence complete, yet not a deathly, chilly silence, but a friendly silence broken only by the calls of grouse, peewits, and other birds, and the rustlings of insects in the long grasses. Worries seem so trivial among all the silent vastnesses and one can almost feel the effect of the fine air as it is breathed in. I think folks with too high an opinion of themselves, ought to spend at least a week alone on our moors, in the redwoods of California, or by the Zambesi Falls, where they would see something bigger and grander than themselves, which would put them in their proper place, and make them realize what miserable specimens they were! If Mussolini had our fine Yorkshire moors near his home, he would never have entered the war.

This house is about three miles from my old home (which I have sold) and lies in a lovely valley. As I write I look out onto a rose garden. A thrush is on the top of a big tree singing beautifully. He keeps pausing to say 'You see you see,' and I do see, clumps of yellow crocuses and chionrodoxas, beautiful green grass, and a huge bed of wallflowers which I hope will be out before I leave. Wall flowers are SO English. A rose which I gave them (a cutting from a vine outside my front door) is full of bud and the leaves smell delicious in the wetness. Apart from sweetbriar, it is the only rose with scented leaves that I know.

A friend whose home is by a costal town told me this week that the Germans dropped over 600 incendiary bombs in and around the hospital. They always go for hospitals. They like to inflict all the agony they can. I certainly hope our people will retaliate all they can, but that they will let all hospitals alone. I was against bombing civilians in the beginning, but after all I have seen, I would like the RAF to bomb anywhere just once and the Germans would give in. I wonder if they realize that Hitler told the German people that no British airplane could ever penetrate into Germany? It would be fine to show some of them who do not know yet the damage our RAF has done, what they can do.

April 4, 1941

Yesterday I went before the censor at Liverpool with all my missionary books and lantern slides: Later in the day when I finally went back to the censor's office to collect my belongings, they said they'd enjoyed their day. My matter was so entirely different from anything they usually had. The chief was most enthusiastic about the slides, wishing it had been possible to hear the lectures. The cases are now tied round with string and two red official's seals thereon. They were objects of great interest to other travelers when I came back at night. I am wondering if they will be mistaken for 'official documents' and it will be a sort of open sesame for me when traveling.

We are having nightly raids now, and sometimes in the daytime, too. I was caught in town one day. I've never been out before in a warning. Everybody went about their business and shopping as if nothing had happened, the only difference being that the fire watchers were on the tops of all the buildings. It looked very strange to see all these people up there in broad daylight. I thought about being a fire watcher on top of a New York skyscraper. Not for me, thank you! Mercifully, a raid did not develop and I was quite startled when the 'Raiders past' signal was given. I had forgotten all about them. However, the Germans made up for it at night, keeping many people better than themselves awake for seven hours.

It is lovely to see the trees and shrubs coming out so quickly. There is quite a big difference each day. Spring is very late this year, but I am glad that my last sight of lovely little England should be when everything is bursting into life again. The birds are all singing so lustily. I have been listening to a lovely little bird in the garden – so much nicer to listen to than gunfire and exploding bombs.

April 19, 1941

I am fired with a great desire to visit your aquarium in New York, to hear the New York Philharmonic Orchestra in the flesh instead of on gramophone records. Last week Mr. B was giving me a musical treat – they have some lovely records – and one of them was the orchestra just mentioned. He looked at me most seriously and said: 'You lucky thing, you'll be able to hear that in person soon, while we must content ourselves with records.'

I should also like to visit Radio City Music Hall, but art galleries leave me cold. Museums with old china and glass I revel in, but the most beautiful pictures ever painted never seem to me to have exactly the right colors for their flowers, trees, or grass.

Winston Churchill announced in the House of Commons that the Italians had captured some British bombs which the Italians themselves were going to drop on Vatican City to make it look as though the British had broken their word not to bomb it. Our airmen have all had strict orders not to touch Vatican City, but I believe Rome is to be bombed. Time it was, too. The Italians used to be a kindly race but they are rapidly being turned into a brutal lot like their German masters.

I understand that Hitler has prophesied that the war will be over this year. Well, it does not rest entirely with him. Things are very serious in the Balkans at the moment, but that does not necessarily mean that everyone will give into him.

The longer the war lasts, the more I am reminded of ancient history when the Germans before the time of Christ displayed the same brutal tactics they do now. I console myself with the thought that brute force and evil methods always defeat their own ends, and though we have to endure horrors untold, they will end sometime and those of us who are left will have to try to evoke a world of kindness and consideration for other nations as well as our own.

April 20, 1941

A lovely Sunday morning. The daughter of the house, my 'adopted niece,' took me for a five or six mile tramp across a shoulder of the moor along footpaths away from main roads, past one or two old halls hundreds of years old with lovely mullioned windows, weathered grey stone tiles, and old oaken doorways. The sort of old houses that are really England. We went through woods where sheets of bluebells will soon be seen. The streams were full of crystal clean water, which by the time it had passed through Sheffield (having joined the Sheaf and the Don) would be a filthy yellow-grey. Overhead there were great banks of glorious clouds against which the branches of the trees looked like lace. Many of the trees were tipped with green. From a distance, they had a dainty feathery appearance against the browny purple of the still bare trees. I'm afraid I'm not very good at descriptions, but I do wish I could make you see it all. It is so beautiful. The sunshine of the last few days has brought things on very quickly, especially the daffodils in the garden.

Most of the houses around here have pretty gardens, some of the big ones are a joy to look at. After the dreary winter and the blackouts, the daffodils, or chalice cups as they were called long ago, seem to me to be extra yellow this year. The smell of the pines and the larches in the warm sun was most invigorating. There was a fine view of the moors stretching as far as the eye could see, blue in the distance, purply brown and green on the nearer parts. We could have been able to forget the war altogether if it had not been for the sound of machine guns and rifle fire with the zoom of a plane overhead, which we took to be ours so we did not lie flat or take cover. The firing was practice by our own men.

I expect sometime when I hear a plane in New York I shall suddenly drop flat in the street or turn in to a doorway, out of sheer force of habit. If I drop flat, it will cause a sensation, and no doubt I shall get myself arrested for drunkeness and disorderliness! In which case, I hope the British consul will speedily bail me out, or whatever it is you do over there when people have been wrongfully arrested.

April 27, 1941

'Oh, to be in England now that April's here.' I don't think the poet would have said that this year. The wind has been terribly cold this last month and this morning we have had snow showers. In spite of the bitter winds the trees are struggling to put out green fingers, all except the ash tree, which surely ought to be the emblem of prudence, for it never shows a sign of green until all the cold biting winds have gone. Then the warm sunshine kisses the sleeping buds into smiling wakefulness and before you know where you are, the whole tree is covered with its beautifully shaped leaves. The cherry and almond trees, like impulsive young folks, cannot wait any longer and are opening odd flowers here and there on the branches, which remind me of small children playing 'hidey', and opening one eye surreptitiously to have a look.

Last night we had a three and a half hour raid. The sirens wailed long and luguburiously as I was almost ready for bed. As I dislike being thwarted, I decided to get into bed and see – or to be more exact – hear what happened. I soon heard all right. The bombers sounded heavily loaded and as if it was hard going. In a few minutes things got to happening and bedlam was let loose. Even in the middle of it all I could not help smiling to hear the 'Jerry's' engines speed up and fly as fast as they could. I must admit had I been in their place, I too should have put on all possible speed for our guns let fly with a vengeance and what a row! After a time I was unable to distinguish between bombs and guns. But it was interesting to listen to the sounds that different kinds of guns made. I was terribly sleepy and every time I managed to doze off there was a terrific bang to wake me up. I consoled myself that I was nice and warm in bed and that the blighters up above were finding it too hot for their comfort and I would be far from sleepy.

There has been a plane about for the past hour. I am tired of getting up to look if it is ours or not. In any case, if it is NOT we shall soon know. It seemed very strange last night, when the sirens wailed their warnings, for me to continue undressing and getting into bed, for in my own home I had promptly to prepare the house for casualties, before the wailing was over, the battle was on, my splints and bandages were ready and in a few moments all preparations were complete. I could, of course, not go to bed. Soldiers do not sleep at their posts, neither do the workers of the Women's Voluntary Service Corps, Housewives Service. I could not help wondering if my former home was safe.

If I look out of the window here – a habit to which I am prone – there is a glorious forsythia in bloom on the lattice work. Its yellow bells seem to ring a cheery message of hope that spring really is coming, and we shall welcome it all the more for its delay.

That blessed plane is so low that the table is vibrating. It looks like a foreign one. There are many fighting in our air force. Perhaps the pilot is friendly with some girl in this district and is showing off a bit! Who can blame him?

April 29, 1941

479 Whirlowdale Road, Sheffield, England

I am back again in my old district. There is a magnificent view from the windows, but unfortunately every window in the house has been treated with antisplinter stuff in case of raids. They are awful to look through, make you feel quite dizzy. Even windows remind us of the war. You cannot get away from war for a second. All trams and bus windows are pasted over with fine black net, to prevent splintering in air raids, with the result that no one can possibly see out, and unless you know the bus route very well, you have no idea where you are, as beside being splinter proof, the windows are also view proof. It is quite comical at times to see the efforts people make to find out where they are. Here the windows have been treated with some chemical solution – the effect is truly awful.

I went to the shipping company this morning. There is every hope that I may get away in May. I have to go before the American consul and then all formalities are completed. I have made my will and given the bank power of attorney, so there is no more business of that kind to see to.

I expect many Americans listened to Winston Churchill last night. He put new cheer into us all. If the USA is going to enter the war, I hope I can get there before she does. I hope it will not be necessary for her to take such a drastic step.

May 2, 1941

I have a contract with a paper here to send a weekly 700 words, but if I meet really interesting people I'm to 'spill the beans'. I do not want an interview such as a reporter gets, but an invitation to a cup of tea – or the American equivalent – and a friendly chat. My articles will very definitely NOT be political, but are to be from a woman's point of view. I shall keep my eyes and ears open for anything of interest to my readers. Also *My Garden*, a 'super' magazine, has arranged to take articles on American gardens from the point of view of a visitor, and not that of a scientist.

You have no idea how war upsets things. There is nothing doing here in literary lines unless it is war books. Several publishing houses have been bombed and millions of books have been destroyed.

May 5, 1941

Last night for the third night running we had ███████ hours of bombing. It began at ███████ and lasted until ███████ spasmodically. I refused to get up, though every time I dozed off there was either a bomb or guns or both to rouse me up again.

Mr. Menzies, the Australian Prime Minister, said last night that the thing which impressed him most over here was the calm steadfastness of the British people.

Hitler wants the British exterminated from the earth. No doubt many of us will be before the end of the war, but all that democracy stands for, and the good and beauty of our country will still live on. I am a great believer in the fact that evil ultimately defeats its own ends. Meanwhile we carry on.

NOTE: *On 10 May 1941, the Deputy Führer of the Third Reich, Rudolf Hess, left Germany in a private plane and parachuted out over Scotland, just south of Glasgow. He was concerned about the possibility of Germany waging a two-front war and hoped to discuss peace possibilities with the British government. He was quickly captured by a Scottish farmer and turned over to the authorities and imprisoned. Hitler ordered him to be shot on sight if he ever returned to Germany. He never did.*

May 18, 1941

I do not see why we should all jump to the conclusion that Germany is cracking up just because of the appearance of one man, (Hess), from that country. People might as well say that England is suing for peace just because a few pacifists here and there proclaim their views from the rooftops. I'm afraid we have a long way to go yet before

Germany falls to pieces. Meanwhile their savage bombing continues. Some lovely buildings have been destroyed, among them a fourth century building, one of the lovely old places of England's pride. On a peaceful, lovely day such as this, it is almost impossible to believe the horror of the nights

I am sitting in the garden chalet. A magnificent view is before me. A great blue shoulder of the moors in the distance, with everywhere you turn trees of every believable, yes, and unbelievable shade of green. (Bother it, a beastly plane droning away, suspiciously heavy, and I have a good way to run to the house if it is necessary to run. I shall stay here and see what happens.)

A little way from me are the fruit trees with their first blossoms of white, palest pink, and deepest pink just showing. (Bang! I don't know where!) On the other side of the garden are some Japanese cherries, flowering almonds, Siberian crabs, Prunuses and forsythias, here and there some blue Cupressus which at this distance look dark and velvety among the reddish brown foliage of the crabs. In the sunken rose garden, the fountain is playing and the sound of the water falling into the pool is delicious. Large tufts of mauve Aubretia hanging down the terrace wall, are reflected in the water where presently water lilies, white, yellow, and red, will float. The scent of sweetbriar is occasionally wafted in to me and a couple of cock blackbirds are having a fight just outside the chalet. A handsome thrush is collecting food to take to its nest and in all the tremendous vista before me I can only see the roof of one house appearing out of the woods. It is very lovely here. Sheffield is surrounded by some of the loveliest country in the British Isles.

The *Daily Mail* announced that 'All mails from the United States dating from March 31 and April 5 and correspondingly earlier dates, (whatever they may mean), have been destroyed by enemy action.' So if anybody wrote to me then I shan't get it. I am going to send this by airmail to see if it will reach you any sooner.

I am glad to notice that your *Saturday Evening Post* has abandoned its isolation policy.

May 23, 1941

When I come to the land of bustle, great rivers, skyscrapers, unlimited onions, and fruit, to say nothing of the wonderfully kind people, do remember to ask me for my recipe for Damson jam and Damson cheese. You'll love them.

Yesterday afternoon I had the honor to speak to the Forty Five club. This is a club composed of workers who knit as hard as they can for the forces. They raise money by all sorts of means and send things to the troops. Yesterday they had a lovely wireless, which they were sending to our forces in Iceland. They were awfully nice to me. (Of course, I couldn't take a fee in the circumstances.) They gave me a message to American women and a number of patterns for standard things required for the forces. All easy to knit and with full instructions, I propose to bring these with me and perhaps some readers who are knitting for England might be glad to have them.

Poor Doris rang me up to tell me that their house had all but collapsed in a recent raid, but they are still cheerful and are making a game of walking across a bedroom floor that is ready to let them down. Her brother said, after all the locks had been blown off the doors, that perhaps now they would get the front door lock altered. It had always been awkward!

I met an old lady of eighty-six at the Forty Five club who is a great bridge player. In a recent raid she happened to be playing when a warning sounded. The family wanted her to go into the shelter and pointed out that the bombs were dropping nearer than seemed pleasant. 'Bombs dropping,' quoth she, 'well, let them. It's my turn to bid and I'm not going to let the Germans stop me.' And they didn't. She played on.

I had a nice letter this week from Miss Comstock, a reader living in Dover, Delaware.

I shall cable, if possible, the day before sailing, but shall not be able to mention the name of the boat, indeed I shall not know it until after we have left land. But you will be able to learn from the Cunard offices, when we should arrive.

All the excitement about Rudolph Hess has died down and the nation has returned to its onion growing, etc., and getting on with the war. He was one of the evil gang and has many foul deeds to his record, but what a compliment to this country. The very country he tried to bring to disaster is the only one he dare flee to, or Hitler's vile Gestapo would have him in their clutches in no time, but he prefers the British and Britain to anywhere else in Europe. We usually treat our enemies fairly, but it is very hard not to get revengeful. When the Germans bomb our hospitals, women and children, it does not frighten us into submission, but rouses us to fury.

Lord Mottistone told this story at a London war weapons week meeting yesterday: A British trawler was successful in shooting down a dive bomber and someone was sent from the Admiralty to inquire from the captain how it was that they were so successful in the encounter. The captain, pointing to George his gunner, replied: 'I sez "George."' He sez: 'Aye, aye sir.' Then I sez: 'Aeroplane reported.' He sez: 'Aye, aye sir.' Then I sez: 'Shoot the blighter.' He sez: 'Aye, aye sir' then shoots him.

May 24, 1941

None of your letters of November, December and January have arrived. They never will now.

The cold is awful. It has been trying to snow this afternoon. M— and I are going to the city to shop. I keep finding one thing and another that I need, yet always forget every time I go, such as a sponge and a new toothbrush.

For the first time since the war began I did not hear the warning at 1 a.m. although the 'all clear' woke me later. Now the nights are moonlit, or supposed to be, we may expect nightly visitations. Our men seem to have found a more satisfactory way of dealing with night bombers. They shot down forty-five in a few nights. To me, a mere woman, it is more than marvelous how they can bring them down at all. For apparently quite often they can't see the planes, but have to be guided by sound. The other afternoon, Robert, my cousin, and I went out to watch the gunfire, really, but ostensibly to look for incendiary bombs and it looked as if every single star and planet in the universe were shining brightly. We could hear the planes so low we wondered if they would clear the tops of the trees, yet we couldn't get a sight of any of them, not even in the light of bursting shells. In fact, it was only judging by the direction of the 'ghost' searchlights and the gunfire that we realized that they were practically overhead. Then we sought shelter under cover of a small roofed courtyard outside the kitchen door. Eventually the bitter cold wind drove us indoors; as we were not on duty, we fortunately could go in if we wanted to. But I was very sorry for all the folk on duty. The wind made you feel as if you had nothing on, however well wrapped up you were.

May 26, 1941

I had an airmail letter from a woman in Dundee asking for news of her niece and family in Sheffield. It only took twelve days to come. I will see what I can do, but in a city nearly the size of New York, it is not easy to trace people entirely unknown to you. I shall write to them as I live a very long way away from some of them. If the houses are still standing I might go several times and not find anyone in, but a letter should reach them even if they have evacuated and the houses are closed or bombed.

We have had rain for the last day or two, and the trees are nearly full out. The coloring is glorious. I began to count the different shades of green of the trees surrounding this garden alone and when I got up to over fifty, I lost my place and had to begin over again, but I never completed the list, for there was always something else interesting to attract the attention.

The bluebells are a carpet in the glen at the bottom of the garden. There will be acres upon acres of bluebells in the woods round about here. A soft, misty blue carpet, with a deliciously delicate scent wafted on the breeze. I think the bluebells look extra lovely when carpeting a wood, with the great trees towering above them, and as the land slopes this way and that, the indescribably beautiful greens of the young beech leaves, reddish yellow sycamore, light red oak, and the soft yellow green of the limes, form a perfect background for the trunks of the silver birches rising out of the endless mass of blue flowers.

Once more, Americans, let me assure you we are not starving, we are not even miserable. Certainly we don't like being bombed and having land mines and incendiary bombs descending on us from above, but we shall keep on keeping on.

May 27, 1941

I was most interested to read about all the grapefruit, oranges, and so forth being gathered. My mouth watered so much I nearly dribbled! I do hope all the lovely fruits you have won't be eaten up when I arrive. Do save me some! It is a fruitless England now, as far as imported fruits go. Ships are needed to bring munitions, war weapons and war materials, so we must do without grapefruit, pineapples, bananas, (which always taste to me like warm darning wool), and very few oranges. I am looking forward to plenty of fruit when I come to the USA. I have always longed to pick oranges off the trees and eat them straight away, pineapples off the plant, peaches off the tree and so on. But I don't suppose that can be done in all parts of the states.

NOTE: *On 27 May 1941, the British Navy sank the German battleship, Bismarck. It was the pride of the German fleet and the largest battleship that Germany had made. Breaking out of the straits near Denmark, Bismarck sank the British battleship* Hood *in the North Atlantic. That was their largest warship. What followed was a chase through the North Atlantic until the British Navy finally destroyed Bismarck, taking 115 of its sailors prisoner.*

May 28, 1941

All Britain was thrilled to the marrow to hear of the sinking of the *Bismarck*. The first lord of the admiralty announced it thus wise: '... It has always been the practice of the British navy to avenge a loss such as that of the *Hood* and at 11 o'clock this morning the *Ark Royal* sighted the *Bismarck*, which has been sunk.' The rest of his speech, (he was speaking at a luncheon in London), was lost in the cheers, yells, clapping, and stamping of excitement of his hearers. I thought it would smash the microphone. By the way the first lord of the admiralty; A. V. Alexander, is member of parliament from Hillsbro', a division of Sheffield, and though he is a Labour member, he is well respected by those of us who are not of his political opinions. I like to hear him speak for he is a direct contrast to Winston Churchill, who is intense and very dramatic when speaking, whereas Mr. Alexander is almost laconic.

May 31, 1941

A beautiful spring morning. I have been wandering around the garden collecting flowers for the house. Among them a 'posy' of small flowers, a ring of ditto, and some bigger, wide spreading effects.

I discovered some exquisite Viburnam, completely hidden from the house, a mass of exotic scented flowers which I gathered. Why are some people so shortsighted as to refuse to cut their flowering shrubs and trees? Properly cut, it is an excellent form of pruning.

I have arranged some Solomon's Seal or Ladder to Heaven, in the wall vase in the lounge. I strip all the leaves off one side and gather it before it is fully out. We have had this a week and it is lovely still. If gathered when fully out, it drops so quickly. It goes so well with the cream walls and 'bluey' green and white curtains. The maids are going away for the weekend as it is Whitsuntide, a great time here usually. War takes no account of these things and we shall not have much in the way of celebrations, but if it is fine and warm there will be thousands of hikers, cyclists, and so forth, making for the country. It will do them a lot of good after such a long, cold, hardworking, air raiding winter.

We are all wondering why we have received so little night attention from Germany lately. We wonder if they are preparing a tremendous onslaught. We don't want it of course, but if it has to come we all feel, 'Well, come, you won't get it all your own way.'

According to the statements of the *Bismarck* prisoners, they were expecting rescue from 200 Luftwaffe planes, which failed to appear. If the Germans can't even keep promises to their own men, who then can trust them?

June 2, 1941

How sad about Crete. If only American help could have reached us many months ago we could have held out. There seems absolutely no end to the Nazis themselves and the powers that be do not care how many lives are lost. Hitler and company always keep themselves well out of the firing lines. It is only their own miserable shirts about which they are so careful.

There is still no definite news about my sailing for America.

I am giving a talk on Thursday. All my notes and books are packed and sealed with official seals so I shall have to speak without reference or preparation.

You say you have had several inquiries for my recipe for raspberry jam. It might be a good idea to repeat it for those who missed it last year: Yorkshire Raspberry Jam – One and one-fourth pounds of fine white sugar to one pound raspberries. Heat sugar in oven and place in deep bowl with alternating layers of raspberries. Beat steadily (the same way round) with wooden spoon for half an hour. Pour at once in stone jars (not glass). Store in cool dark place. If properly made it will keep for months. W. M. G.

It is time I went in and changed for tea. Don't forget we in England keep on keeping on and are still far from starving.

NOTE: *On 22 June 1941 Hitler violated his Non-Aggression Pact and launched what he called Operation Barbarossa, the invasion of the Soviet Union. In a few days, Great Britain signed an alliance with the Soviets, which created a two-front war for the Germans. Usually strictly anti-communist and a critic of Stalin, Churchill famously said: 'If Hitler invaded hell I would make at least a favourable reference to the devil in the House of Commons.'*

July 3, 1941

The Russians seem to be holding their own. The general feeling here is that if they hold out against Germany, Hitler's doom is nearer than we thought. If they don't manage it, then there will be fewer planes, tanks, guns, and men to hurl against us, and that's all that anyone bothers.

Last afternoon there was a 'gas practice' in this district. They let off some powerful smelling stuff, that would do no harm of course, but enabled wardens, police, firemen, ambulance first aid, Women's WVS, etc., all to practice what they would have to do in a real gas raid. As usual some very funny things happened. The heat was terrific and the poor things had to wear their decontamination suits which admit no more air than a diving suit, tin hats, gas masks, etc. The casualties thought they would have the best of it, as they were labeled and laid out on the pavement. Later it was found they had been labeled on their backs and had to be turned over before the ambulance corps knew what they were or where to take them.

The 'casualties' found out they were not so well off after all, for the pavements were scorching hot and breathing through a gas mask at any time is no fun, but lying flat on their backs with their 'swine's snouts' up in the air was suffocating. There was no air and if they laughed, it used up too much air in the masks. We were terribly hot in thin frocks and no masks. As the wind blew the gas the other way, we were able to laugh at the victims.

I am utterly weary. After several sleepless nights owing to the awful heat, we were roused at ██████ . Mrs. G. came into my room where I was hurriedly dressing. The casement windows were wide open and it was literally impossible to hear ourselves speak. I hung out of the windows to try and see the planes, but although it was a full moon, the sky was one big grey canopy (mercifully.) Never in all our raids have I heard so many planes; the row was TERRIFIC. We felt that with all that noise, we ought to see them clearly. The city and suburbs were empty and silent. A few minutes later, this road was swarming with wardens running down to their stations, fire watchers patrolling, and first aid folk at strategic points. It seemed so strange to me to be in the midst of it all again and yet have no responsibilities.

Mrs. G. is fearfully nervous and I saw I was going to have something to do! Unfortunately, I felt so terribly irritable and knew I must be 'calm, cool, careful and resourceful' according to the training instructions. I've never dressed so fast in a raid and came down without my gas mask and warm coat. 'O dear me, what are we going to do?' she asked. 'Come on,' I said, 'We'll play rummy.' I'm afraid I was rather bossy. She wanted to go out and look, so against all regulations, I let her and went with her. I thought if she saw for herself that all was all right around, she might settle down. She knew two women across the road and they came across and talked. Finally we decided to come in and they came too and I taught three people rummy. We played for two hours. She got so absorbed, she forgot to dither and every time we heard the planes going over, I lied boldly that it was a military lorry or dispatch rider going by, meanwhile treading hard on the feet of the other two. As neither of them had stockings on and one of them only light sandals, the pressure I brought to bear was effective. They calmly went on playing without comment on the noises or my lie, or the unpleasant proximity of my high heeled shoes, the only ones I could find quickly in the dark.

For once I acted on the principle so beloved by the Germans – use a lie, a thumping one, to gain your end. Now and again a warden appeared. 'Are you ladies all right?' We had tea and biscuits and I gave the warden who came in a cup. He wanted to join us in rummy, but we shooed him out to his duty. (He did not take much shooing.) I hope the recording angel will deal gently with me, but everyone was much more comfortable than if I had said: 'Can you hear those planes?'

When 'Raiders Past' sounded, we rose as one man – or woman – and without a word they made for the door, said goodnight, and were gone. I put the cards away, Mrs. G. came back, we said good morning at ▮▮▮▮▮▮▮ and parted.

At 2 p.m. we heard of the signing of the pact with Russia. As this country is violently anti-communist, there is no wild enthusiasm over it, just a feeling that whoever is Hitler's enemy is our ally and to be treated accordingly. I only hope the Russians will not ultimately let us down. They are doing very well up to the present time.

> **NOTE:** *A humanitarian organisation named Bundles For Britain started in New York City in 1940 and spread across the United States. A chapter formed in Yates County in November of that year to 'receive woolen articles of clothing to be sent to England to assist in supplying much-needed winter wearing apparel for the homeless hundreds of that war-torn country'. Using a room in the Arcade Building on Main Street in Penn Yan as a headquarters, they collected knitted goods and other articles of clothing. Labels were sewn on the knitted garments stating, 'From Your American Friends.' They continued activities until June of 1942.*

July 27, 1941

9 Edale Road, Sheffield, England

I have been given facilities for visiting all the various activities of Women's Voluntary Service corps, Civil Defense. I went to the central clothing depot where ladies were sorting whole outfits of clothes for people. They told me boys' underclothing was especially needed from 5 years old to 15 years. Boys' clothing of any sort, especially underwear, also girls' underwear.

One ladies' organization sent a most magnificent assortment of baby clothes. Lady Gibson said they were 'wonderful' and when one poor soul received some of the lovely garments for her baby, tears rolled down her cheeks and she said, 'Oh, aren't the American ladies kind! You will thank them, won't you?' So I pass on the message, for America has responded right well to our appeals. Lady

Gibson said to me that the American ladies seemed as if they could not do enough for us. 'Just splendid they are! Mind you tell them so.' You see if a town within reasonable reach is badly bombed, then the other towns which have escaped at that particular moment all rush help and supplies to the victims. Some of the things received here have been used in that way as well as among our own citizens.

Then another time I went to a center run entirely by volunteer help. It was opened after our blitz. Many of the men and women workers have gone every day since then and a jolly good mid-day meal, well cooked, plenty of it, and spotlessly clean it all is. I went and got my tray and food and went and sat among the workers while I had it. I told them I was coming to America and asked for messages to your great nation.

> 'Tell them to hurry up with the planes.'
> 'Tell them to send us the goods and we'll do the job.'
> 'Tell them to shoot that ★★★★★★ swine, Lindbergh.'
> 'Tell them we've got plenty to eat.'
> 'Tell them to send us some fruit.'
> 'Ask them to send us some cigarettes.'

I told them I wasn't sure what could be done about the cigarettes on account of duty and so forth. One man had been bombed out and said: 'Thank the ladies who sent us such lovely things for the kids. We shan't forget it.' Another man who had received help said: 'If ever America wants help when this war is over, I'll help.' It was certainly touching at times to see their cheerfulness, their determination to carry on, their absolute certainty we were going to win, their utter contempt for Mussolini, and their sheer inability to think of Hitler and Company as anything else than a band of evil madmen to be exterminated when, where, and how as ever Churchill sees fit! When I said: 'Are we downhearted?' the yell of 'NO' nearly burst my eardrums.

NOTE: *Charles Lindbergh, the aviation hero of the 1920s, was a strict isolationist who was accused of being a fascist sympathiser in 1941. He became a major spokesman for the America First Committee and maintained that America should stay out of the European war.*

July 30, 1941

The other day I bought a map of the USA which I hope our officials will allow us to bring! The scale is 120 miles to the inch, but it gives me a rough idea of where places are. The great city of Penn Yan is not marked! It was only shortly before I left that I discovered Washington was on the Atlantic side and not Pacific side like I had supposed! I was greatly relieved to find another Washington over there so I was not entirely wrong.

Dr. Gager of Brooklyn has sent a personal message to the Cunard Company over here asking them to see that I get passage in time for the lecture! I've sent a copy to the passport office as well. I've been bombarding them with letters. If they fail to produce a response, I shall go to London, but traveling in these islands is much discouraged and such trains as there are are not run with the idea of encouraging folk to tear about on anything but vital government concerns.

I don't know what on earth I can have said for the censor to cut out, tiresome war, but I'd rather he cut the letters to bits than that I should give anything away. I don't see how I can give anything away. I don't know anything except what is happening to us here. I don't know what the Germans have been saying about Sheffield, according to cousin Jessie's letter it must have been one or more of their selected lies guaranteed to throw dust in the eyes of American people. Anyhow don't believe them ever. Please get rid of the idea that we are starving – we are not. True there are some fruits we cannot get, but we have equal distribution of food, and British, Jews, Germans, Japanese, etc., are all treated alike. Whatever their nationality they get the same rations as the rest of us. Everyone in the British Isles gets their weekly ration without fail.

By the way when I was giving you a few messages from the workers at the canteen I visited, one of them said, 'Give our love to Dorothy Thompson, the finest woman in the world.' If it is ever my privilege to meet her I must give it to her.

NOTE: *Dorothy Celene Thompson (9 July 1893–30 January 1961) was an American journalist and political commentator. She was a prominent opponent of Hitler and fascism, which led to her being the first American journalist to be expelled from Nazi Germany in 1934. In 1939 Thompson was recognised by* Time Magazine *as the second most influential woman in America next to Eleanor Roosevelt; she is regarded by some as the 'First Lady of American Journalism'.*

August 12, 1941

We are wondering what the Germans are up to as we have had a spell of comparatively mild air raids all over the country, if indeed you can call any of them mild. They will probably make savage attacks on us again before long.

This morning it was so peaceful and the weather so beautiful we decided to take a bus trip into the country. By the time we were ready to start, it was pouring, but I insisted upon going. ▆▆▆▆▆▆▆▆▆▆▆▆▆ It poured the whole time, but as soon as we returned and shut the front door, the sun came out and has been shining ever since.

A friend has loaned me an old Herbal 300 years old. The illustrations are marvelous. I love handling old books and wondering about the people who owned them and read and cherished them long ago.

> **NOTE:** *In August 1941, using the cover story that he was going fishing for a week in a yacht off the New England coast, President Roosevelt met with Prime Minister Churchill on an American destroyer off Newfoundland. Churchill hoped to pressure Roosevelt to declare war against Germany. Roosevelt at that time believed American involvement was inevitable, but knew that the strongly isolationist attitude of Congress and the American people would not tolerate it. What the two leaders did was draw up a series of goals for the postwar world. Included was the blueprint for the United Nations. Although the meeting was held in secret, their war aims were released to the public as the Atlantic Charter on 14 August.*

August 15, 1941

There is one thing about being fetched out of bed in the dead of night by air raids, I have got quite a lot of knitting done, which is a great help.

Yesterday I went to the very outskirts of civilization to see some friends. M. took us for a ride in the afternoon and we went right up on the highlands. It was very peaceful but awfully cold and we felt nicely freshened up.

We were all thrilled to learn yesterday that Mr. Winston Churchill and your president have met at sea. I had thought it strange that Mr. Roosevelt should be yachting during such tense times, but I certainly never dreamed what was really happening.

A woman who used to live next door to us on Ringinglow Road met me on a bus the other day and nearly fell off when she saw me, as she had heard I was touring America.

A plane is zooming around overhead. Mrs. G. drew my attention to it. With all the assurance complete ignorance gives, I declared it to be one of ours. I don't know whose it is, but feel if it were an enemy one, someone would do something about it. Besides, there is no point getting hot and bothered about it. The other night some fire wardens were in here and we had an argument as to whether we should rather have daylight or night raids. No agreement was reached. In any case, we shall have to take what comes without choice.

August 21, 1941

Yesterday I went into some very lovely country outside of Sheffield where some friends are staying. It was difficult to think of war with those calm stately hills all about us, large tracts of woodland on the slopes and fields of golden grain in the folds. Grey stone cottages centuries old with soft smoke curling lazily out of the chimneys made a peaceful picture of this typically English countryside.

My young sailor friends were reminiscing not long ago about what they liked to think of when they are on duty at sea in bitterly cold weather. Most of them like to let their fancy roam to this or that piece of countryside where they have spent jolly days (maybe enhanced by some female companionship) – the heather in full bloom in August, the pines putting on their spring dress, a sunset over the moors. One of them told me when he is on watch and hungry, he remembers my sausage rolls (for which I have a mild fame).

J.M. is on leave and came to see me this week. He seemed very well. The friends with whom I am staying liked him very much and we had quite a lively time. He has been promoted now to Leading Signalman and has been sent to another ship. He is at present engaged in very dangerous work about which I'd better say nothing. He seems to enjoy the excitement of it.

Yesterday we saw the films of your president and Mr. Churchill and the audience cheered wildly. Your president is very popular in this country, but let anyone mention Col. Lindbergh!

I am writing an article for my American press agent about the women of England.

I am still struggling with the shipping company about my passage to America. The government has given me permission to go, but the Cunard company is being more than awkward and that is the only line left to the States. I do hope I shall get there in time for my lecture engagement in Brooklyn. I booked passage nearly twelve months ago!

August 31, 1941

During a wakeful night I was interested to watch the stars gliding almost imperceptibly across the open window of my room. The blackout arrangement on this window does not permit me to open it with the light on. As I like to keep it open, it means that in case of a sudden alarm in the night I have to grope around in the darkness. During the night I wondered if the stars would all be in their wrong places when I reach USA – the North Star pointing to the south and Cassiopea upside down!

I have had no mail from your country in a long time. Perhaps it has gone to the mermaids.

September 7, 1941

Today is a day of national prayer. I have just come back from church. Instead of going down into the city to my own Congregational church, I went to the Established (national.) Although we were twenty minutes before time, there was not a seat to be had. They got chairs and put them all over. Finally, we were placed between the choir and organ at right angles to the congregation. It is an 11th century building which has been enlarged to hold the growing congregation. They have built the new part to conform to the old. As there was a twenty foot pillar between me and the pulpit, I heard little of the sermon. The church was packed with soldiers, airmen, wardens, Brownies, women's auxiliary, and all sorts of important people. Most of the officers and men gave up their seats to women and it must have been tiring to stand at attention during the whole service – but how they did sing!

During the sermon, a familiar drone sounded above. I saw two officers look at each other and I wondered what would happen if a bomb dropped on us. But the atmosphere of the place, where people have worshipped for 900 years, seemed to fold one in an invisible blanket of protection and nothing happened.

The other day a friend told me of her parents' experience on the night of the first Sheffield blitz. The old couple in their 70s went and sat on the bottom of the cellar steps. A land mine blew their house flat along with the other houses in the neighbourhood. The explosion blew them up to the top of the cellar stairs, breaking the man's neck and the woman's collar bone. They were buried for nine hours in the ruins. The woman finally made herself heard and the rescue party extricated her with great difficulty, but the man was dead. She was in the hospital for several months, but is now game and just wonderful.

I broke off here to listen to our Princess Royal broadcast appealing for salvage. We are beginning to get many broadcasts from Russia now. The Russians are a determined lot.

September 14, 1941

There still seem to be complications about my getting passage to America. I am now appealing directly to high authority to see if

I can get results. My clothes have been packed since March 29th waiting to sail.

One of my lifelong friends has been bombed out of her home. She was a shelter warden, a WVS, and goodness knows what else and had had no sleep for five nights owing to consecutive raids. So as she is not very young, they persuaded her to go to bed. Then the sirens suddenly sounded, but she was so utterly exhausted she decided to stay put and risk it. She lay there listening to the pandemonium of whistling bombs and roaring guns when there was a deafening crash followed by the disintegration of everything around her. She ducked her head under the bedclothes and thought, 'Now I am going to eternity! I've often wondered what it would be like!' She felt stuff raining down on top of her and after a time she tried to move and found herself uninjured, and yelled out, 'Why, I'm not dead!' Half of the house had been completely demolished, but she got out safely and said, 'Thank goodness it is a fine night.'

Her sister and I met accidentally in town yesterday and had a good laugh over her and a 'chinwag' over our coffee. This house that had been bombed was a very lovely one with beautiful furniture, and after she had checked up on the damage, she indignantly said she didn't think they 'need make such a filthy mess when they bomb us!'

I have volunteered for work at a decontamination center in case of gas raids. If there is no gas I want to do fire fighting. I like something that requires action, and that right promptly. The other day I was caught in the city in a gas attack practice. I've never seen anything so funny as a tram full of people all wearing their gas masks. Women out shopping all calmly carrying their hat along with their handbags and wearing their gas masks all as a matter of course. The sight of the police tickled me mightily as I do not see how they could issue any orders buried in their service masks. Everyone looked like beings from the world of nightmares. At least gas masks, like misfortunes, are great levelers for the handsomest man and most beautiful woman in the world look as ugly as everyone else enveloped in the hideous things!

I am trying to finish a pair of khaki socks today. Tuesday I am going to London to 'beard all the lions in all their dens,' and try to get my passage to America.

October 4, 1941

I wonder when I shall ever see the 'Promised Land' America. I have long been promised I could go, but get a passage by fair means or foul, I cannot. Last Tuesday I penetrated into one of the jealously guarded sanctuaries occupied by certain ministers in London and stated my case. Whether or not this will make any impression, I don't know, but it cheered me up hugely to be able to say something instead of writing cold, courteous letters about the matter.

After I'd done this M. B. (who had come to London with me) and I went to Westminster Abbey as I wanted to see the 'Unknown Warrior's' grave. (Did you read Morton's book *In Search of England?*) There was much less apparent air raid damage to the abbey than we had dared to hope. Big Ben stood erect keeping a watchful face on the busy world below. The dear old abbey with St. Margaret's and the Houses of Parliament stood there in such a dignified way it gave us a sense of everlasting security. 'The heart of the empire' was calm and dignified as ever. We stood on Westminster bridge and watched 'Old Father Thames' glide silently by on his way to the North Sea. The remains of St. Thomas' hospital on the banks bore the marks of bestial German warfare for all to see.

We took a taxi to St. Paul's. I've never cared about it before but this time I couldn't help falling deeply in love with it. Bomb-scarred and damaged, it stood erect above the wreckage all about. The altar was demolished, but the great dome was unharmed. Large blocks of masonry had fallen and remained intact. The carving in the choir stalls and the wonderful woodwork seemed to be undamaged, though the twelve apostles looked a bit disreputable with dusty beards.

As we stood there in the dark cathedral with boarded windows a soft gold light from the afternoon sun shone through the dome and lit up the stone figures high up in their niches, giving the saints an unusually pleasant expression. It was almost a heavenly light, and we who stood far beneath seeing it felt that the old church with its great grandeur was quietly reassuring us that there would once again be peace and happiness for us all.

October 5, 1941

The appeal I sent to relatives in California for baby clothes was passed on to various organizations and they are sending consignments direct to Sheffield as I suggested. I rang up Lady Gibson, the head of the WVS to tell her and she was pleased.

Although we cannot often get imported fruits now we have plenty of food and our rations are soon to be increased. There is no shortage of coffee whatever.

October 13, 1941

It is just after lunch, during which, we listened to a 'Workers Playtime' concert. It is put on by various factories and often world famous artists take part. There is no end of talent among the factory workers themselves, especially in the North. It is strange, but nearly all the greatest comedians come from the North, Yorkshire and Lancashire, with Scotland close behind. When workers themselves broadcast from northern factories we know we are in for a good laugh.

It was very cold last night. I took a hot bath and went to bed with a hot water bottle but had only been there about five minutes when the air raid warning sounded and up I had to get.

October 16, 1941

The book I am reading about New York City says that your skyscraper lifts go at a speed of 1,200 feet a minute and that it often affects the ankles of stout folk and the backs of thin ones. I hope I shall not have a broken back as soon as I reach your mighty shores. Someone said not long ago that the middle of a skyscraper was safer than the top or bottom in an air raid! I fail to see how if the top or bottom are wrecked, there would be any middle.

I was interested in the picture of the stone lions in front of the New York Public Library. They look so gaunt; our Trafalgar Square lions are such regal well-fed creatures guarding Nelson up on his monument as he looks toward the Admiralty buildings. The contrast struck me forcibly. I am looking forward to seeing your buildings. I cannot yet say definitely when I am sailing. I am sorry to be so awkward, but we are not allowed to give information that might tell the U-boats where we are going at a given time.

Last night when coming home in the tram after blackout, I let down a window and admired the silhouettes of the buildings against the sky as we passed. An artist could paint a beautiful picture of the moonlit sky and the long fingers of many searchlights groping in the banks of clouds for enemy planes. Even the wrecked buildings of a darkened city have a beauty of line against the starry sky. Such pictures would appeal to me far more as something to remember of this war than those of wounded civilians, dead children, and headless bodies of people lying in the streets. We who have seen these things do not need pictures to remind us. The memory of ghostliners is burnt into the very souls of men and women of all European countries

October 17, 1941

I had occasion to go into the city and, owing to a heavy downpour, took shelter in a shop doorway. Two young airmen did the same. I thought at first they were British and then heard one of them speaking in a foreign language and saw an emblem on his breast with the word Poland. I had an impulse to shake his hand and say 'Long Live Poland!' but being British, I only looked at it and smiled at him. He was only a boy and had such a nice face and appearance that I would have thought him British, (I am told that when I come to America I must not use this sort of compliment i.e. to say about an American that he, or she, is so nice one might think he were English!)

I hope the magazines and papers I send arrive safely. There is an article about the desecration of churches in Greece and Crete by the Germans. Try to imagine anything like that happening in America. Even your isolationists would not like it.

A young pilot-to-be offered me a dud incendiary bomb that fell by his garden wall to bring to USA to be auctioned for the British War Relief funds! I told him I had had enough trouble to secure passage without packing a dud bomb in my luggage and risking an explosion, although he assured me he had tested it by hitting with a hammer and it would not go off. So he has decided to have it refilled and take it back to Germany when he finishes his training!

I am still taking embroidery lessons and have finished my second miniature. Miss Williams, the instructress, deserves most of the credit as she can turn what looks like a mass of badly cooked spinach into a stately pine with a few deft stitches for accent.

You have probably heard 'Berlin Bertie,' Lord Haw Haw's twin brother. He breaks in by saying 'It's all lies! Mr. Churchill how much he is paid by the Germans.' When the Americans said a U boat had sunk an American vessel he said, 'It was a British submarine!' That sort of thing does not upset us, indeed the Britons find him silly enough to be amusing.

We are all right in spite of what the Germans say — tired, but still carrying on vigorously.

I will try to describe a sky during an air raid. As it might apply to any air raid in any country, I think the censor will let it alone. Imagine a dark blue sky spangled with stars. Search-lights, scores of them, criss crossing with occasional spotlights, vivid blinding flashes (like sheet lightning intensified a thousand times) and gloriously colored balls of light as tracer bullets or shells from British guns burst high. Sometimes these gun flashes can be seen when we cannot hear the guns themselves. It is a magnificent spectacle which I always enjoy watching from the artistic point of view, but underlying it all is the haunting spectre of death or injury for some of my fellow countrymen.

During a recent German performance here six of us were seated at dinner at a large round Britishly-solid table (originally the property of one of our local earls). Suddenly extra loud bangs and heavy gun fire caused every one of us simultaneously to drop from our chairs and seek refuge under the table. This was supported by such a very large solid pillar in the center that there was room for only our heads and shoulders! I suddenly thought what we must all look like sticking out around the table and remarked what a bonny spectacle it must be. We all laughed so much about it we resumed our seats and dinner in spite of the loud noise and heavy gun fire.

I always think the fellows up aloft are more uncomfortable than we are by a long chalk, so let the guns bang.

I was told authentically about a woman of 16 stones sitting in a chair when the blast from a bomb picked up both her and the chair and deposited them on the side of the room. She was shaken, but uninjured. (A stone is 14 pounds.)

I have registered passage with an American shipping company in case I cannot go on a British ship, as planned. I have had permission and my passport given me a month ago, but getting passage on a boat is the stumbling block. I have now appealed to the home secretary.

October 26, 1941

Today we are having a huge 'invasion practice' and all civilians who are about are liable to be commandeered for anything the authorities like to make them do. I should think it would be great fun for those taking part. But even in practice I should not like to take the part of German parachute troops.

In a recent raid we had a queer experience. All sounds of every description had ceased. Five of us sat there and at the moment I was counting the stitches of my knitting, when without any warning whatever there was an appalling crash – the whole house shook, pendant lights swung, and we all rose and fell in our chairs exactly as if we were riding horseback. I remember noticing even while waiting for the house to come down on top of us (which it didn't) how gracefully each one of the party rose and fell in her chair! In the dead silence that followed we all burst out laughing. Each told the other how frightfully funny she looked, it was one of the most amusing sights I have seen during a raid.

Every thing is not always so funny, however. A woman told me about her niece who lives in another town. She has been bombed out twice and is now suffering from 'blast lung' – A lung had burst in an explosion and had to be stitched up.

October 28, 1941

This morning I was horrified and distressed to learn that my embroidery teacher had been burned to death in her own home. I know she will be missed by many as she was so nice, as well as being a marvelous embroidery teacher. I am glad to have had the privilege of even four months with her. I have finished the Renaissance tablecloth I started with her and will bring it to the US with me.

I am knitting a wool frock that I started last winter. It will be a 'triumph' now because we can only buy wool with our clothes coupons and no one has enough to spare for knitting wool for frocks. I find knitting very soothing. A friend of mine tells me the sight of me knitting during an air raid gives her confidence that we shall come out all right – my determination to finish a sailor's helmet so that he could have it at the end of the week, for instance, she found very comforting. If she had known what my knees felt like she might not have felt so cheerful!

We are all very calm on the outside and determined to 'stick it out'.

NOTE: *On 7 December 1941 the Japanese attacked the United States naval base at Pearl Harbor, Hawaii. The next day, the USA entered the war against Japan and its Axis partners. You will notice that there was a long gap between letters after that. There are presumably two reasons for that. First, on the theory that the two cousins, with the cooperation of the editor of the Chronicle-Express, were trying to, in a small way, influence public opinion during the period of neutrality in the USA this became a moot point after 7 December. Secondly, the Chronicle-Express, which had committed a large amount of space to Winifred Graville's letters between 1939 and 1941, shifted over to American war news. Even so, eleven more letters were published as space allowed and gave some interesting insight into the war in 1942.*

September 5, 1942

26 Chatsworth Road, Totley Rise, Sheffield, England

On July 13th I started a depot at the university for receiving, sorting, and drying medicinal plants collected by the public for the National Drug Collecting scheme. The Princess Royal (the king's only sister) came to see us and I was presented to her. She was very sweet and informal and asked a number of questions. Her lady in waiting, who is a very charming woman, stayed with me most of the time. One of the WVS women – a wealthy country woman, but delightful with a sense of humour like unto mine own – told them that I was a 'very entertaining speaker'. The princess asked me what had made me take up such an unusual and interesting subject.

I cannot remember whether I told you about being blown across the road in an air raid. I have had some good laughs over it.

Someone from California recently wrote me that her nephew has come over to England with the US air force. I would get in touch with him only she has given me no address. I only know he is Colonel Ronin. I would try to arrange a meeting if she would give me the address. You see all places or camps, aerodromes, etc., etc., are kept as secret as possible. In this country the need for secrecy about troops, sailors, munition works, etc., is very great. We are so small compared with US and so near Germany, France, Belgium, and Holland that the beastly planes can get at us too easily to let it be generally known where anything vital is. Probably the address will be a non-committal headquarters somewhere and they will be forwarded. I have seen a number of American soldiers (black and white) about.

September 9, 1942

On Friday p.m. a party of us from the boarding house are going to see 'Mary Rose'. As I am a great lover of Barrie, I am looking forward to it muchly – being a mystical play, it will appeal to me.

The paper shortage leads to some funny sights. The things one sees being carried home under the arms or in baskets are mirth provoking at times. I saw a young man carrying his laundry under his arm with one pajama leg fluttering in the breeze behind him as he walked. I carried home one of my frocks from the cleaners over my arm to the enjoyment of a kitten on the pavement who thought the flopping belt was a personal invitation to a game! My shoes I fetched from the cobblers and unblushingly carried them in my hand as though in the house. Everyone has long since ceased to take the slightest notice of what anyone else is carrying. Even the spectacle of a well dressed man leaving an expensive china shop with a piece of bedroom china of the sort usually kept out of sight under the bed, under each arm, hardly causes a smile among the onlookers. Though a member of the WVS did refuse to carry a pair of kippers that the fishmonger would not wrap up. Food is allowed to be wrapped, but it is illegal for shopkeepers to wrap other purchases in paper for customers, who may take their own paper if they like. Most folk carry cases or baskets. It is a bit of a nuisance in wet weather. But we all manage very well and every one makes a joke of it. There is more to worry about than wrapping paper.

I like the American food that I have had so far (in tins). We are lucky in this country to have the food we do. I personally need a great deal more fat and sugar than I get, but I am so thankful that we get decent food at all that I should feel very wicked if I grumbled. We are the best fed nation in Europe. Lord Woolton has really done wonders. At least every one in the country gets their share, and we all have the same amount. I think everyone feels that as long as we all share and share alike, the fact that we have to go without many things that we like just doesn't matter. I like the wartime bread very much and hope it will continue after the war is over. Whenever that may be! It is not exactly brown bread, but it certainly is not white. Too much brown bread before the war did not agree with me.

Shopping nowadays is a great gamble. To find a shop with a few yards of elastic for sale is nearly as good as discovering America was hundreds of years ago! Some things have disappeared completely not to return till after the war. I always suffer a wild surprise when I get what I ask for in the first shop I come to! I am wearing bandy legged hairpins and if I lose a hair grip (called 'bobby pin' in America) like the woman in the Bible who searched for her silver coin, I do ditto! It seems extraordinary to me to realize that saucepans and kettles are unobtainable. I do not envy housewives in these times. But they all seem to get along very well somehow. Of course no private cars (automobiles to you) are running. Petrol is only issued to business folks and then it is very much cut down. It is amazing the difference that taking all the private cars off the roads has made. We can cross the streets anywhere we like in a leisurely fashion if so desired and know that we shall reach the other side safely.

September 17, 1942

The US stamps with anti-aircraft guns on them instead of somebody's head are eagerly pounced upon here. On the rare occasions when I receive a letter from you the stamps are quickly sought by many folk. I give them all to various stamp collectors. You seem to be almost the only one who uses those stamps when writing to me.

We have had an absolute glut of raspberry leaves at the university. Sacks upon sacks of them, and as each leaf has to be examined separately not the five leaves on the subsidiary stalk, but each leaf itself – you can imagine the amount of work. Part of last week I was alone and I worked so hard that when I looked up, everything appeared green and people's faces looked like raspberry leaves! My eyes were very sore and bloodshot, but they are better now.

There isn't much news. I am so afraid of saying something the censor will disapprove of and then mutilate my letter that I daren't say anything. Though I am sure nothing I could say would be of the slightest use to the enemy, as I know only what everyone else knows and what we live through ourselves. If I did know any secrets I would on no account let on – as it is I'm really glad I don't.

None of us consider the clothes coupons enough. There are twenty to last from Oct. 10 till April 25. Five for a pair of boots or shoes, two for pair of stockings, five for knickers, five for contributions, two for shin gloves, 18 for coat, fifteen for dress, and so on. So you can see how difficult it is to make them spin out. Mercifully I am all rigged out for dresses. Three for brassier, five for corsets and so it goes on. Clothes will wear out, however much care you take, and housewives do much patch and darn.

I get plenty to eat even if it is not what I like best. So don't think we are starving. We are not.

September 27, 1942

26 Chatsworth Road, Totley Rise, Sheffield, England

I have now finished my voluntary work at the Herb Drying centre. We have closed down till next year. I was very pleased to receive the gratification of the government department, who said publicly in the South of England that 'the Sheffield Herb Drying Centre was the best run centre in the country and that the dried herbs were of the highest quality.' I am feeling so thankful, because we started without a single bit of apparatus of any kind whatsoever, apart from the bare laboratory benches. If people had not been so kind when I asked for things, and the helpers so willing to be told what to do and how to do it, the whole thing would have been a ghastly failure. One of the most dependable and competent workers, besides being always willing and cheery, was a 14-year-old Boy Scout. He was kind enough to say to me when saying goodbye, 'Oh, Miss Graville, I hope you get torpedoed, and have to come back to England. I don't want you to go to America. We shall never see you again!'

The coupon business hampers my style very much!! Seriously it is very hard. Eighteen for a winter coat, 5 for boots or shoes, 5 for knickers, 5 for corsets, 2 for gloves, 2 for stockings, 6 for combinations, 5 petticoats, etc., etc. We only have 20 to last over six months. Thank goodness I've got enough dresses – they are 15 coupons each – to last me for a time yet, but I cannot get a winter dressing gown as it would take about 12 or more.

The fuel rationing is going to be really hard on many people. I had so hoped to be in the States for the winter. I don't know how I shall get along as I feel the cold terribly indoors. I don't mind so much out of doors; if I go out warm I can usually keep warm by walking. But poor fires and cold rooms nearly finish me.

September 29, 1942

I really dread the winter and the fuel rationing is down to the very minimum, so invalids, old people, and people like myself who can't stand cold are going to have a very thin time. My only hope is that the Germans will be colder still!!! I'm afraid they'll take the coal from the occupied countries for themselves and leave the occupied countries with very little. All of which is no help towards warming us!

Last week I went to see the 'Jungle Book' of the films. It was not in the very least like Kipling's glorious stories, but the coloring was lovely, the animals were fascinating. I always wonder how they manage to film such things. The snakes were very unconvincing, but all the other animals were real. I want to see 'Gone With the Wind', but it is a four-hour show and I don't know when it will reach Sheffield, and too, it will be awkward to fit in.

NOTE: *This entry was in the Brooklyn Botanical Garden Record for September 1942:*

An Herb Garden Day had been projected for September 30, with a lecture by Miss Winifred M. Graville, F. R. PLS. of Sheffield, England, but on account of the international situation, it was impossible for Miss Graville to secure passage to this country and so this affair was cancelled.

October 6, 1942

I went to the films again the other afternoon and saw the authentic picture of the convoy to Russia with war necessities. It was the largest convoy there has ever been, men of all allies sailed in it, Chinese, Americans, British, Dutch, Free French, Norwegians, etc. The Russians themselves said 'that for sheer daring and bravery they have never seen the equal of the British seamen.' We have so much to manage over here [but] still have the fighting spirit of the seamen of days gone by, the men who helped to make our empire. To tell a British sailor that he cannot or must not do a thing is to make him the more determined. I'm like that too, only without the personal bravery. Difficulties are made to be overcome and there is a great joy in overcoming them.

I was recently offered the post of organizing the land army somewhere in England. I would have jumped at it, but for the fact that there was extremely intricate office work to be done. As I've never had any experience of office work at all I regretfully refused. If so much had not been at stake I'd have had a good shot at it.

October 16, 1942

This morning I received notice of a possible passage before so very long. I dare not say when. They do not tell us exactly and it will be

very awkward when I cable as I shall certainly not be allowed to say when I expect to arrive, or when I sail from England.
WINIFRED GRAVILLE.

November 1, 1942

I have a very great longing to visit America and am fully prepared to act on the advice of a much travelled friend who said that if I visited US as a foreign country where English is spoken then I should love it, but if I expected to find another England then I should be terribly disappointed. I don't want to find another England! In fact as far as I am concerned there isn't another England! America has a charm of its own, according to my friend, a charm that will have a great appeal to me.

As for the risk of crossing, it is vastly less dangerous – in that it lasts for so short a time – than vicious bombing attacks. We never know too when we may be badly gassed, and then there is the possibility of invasion, which latter disturbs me not at all, because we are ready for it.

You folk in the US who have never seen a bomb or heard anti-aircraft shells exploding and the shrapnel coming down like tropical rain, who have never dealt with incendiary bombs to save your homes, who have never seen little children's mangled bodies, or friends blown to bits so that even a hair remained, who have never seen whole blocks of buildings crash with one bomb and seen streets and streets of blazing buildings, who have never seen the effects of land mines which make craters anything from 30 to 50 feet deep exploding everything near for many many yards, who have never seen oil torches which make suffocating fumes thus rendering aid to the trapped more difficult, (and God knows it's difficult enough without that), who have never seen aerial torpedoes going through several buildings exploding them on their journey, have never heard the groans and cries for help [of] those trapped in burning or ruined buildings, who have never seen the ghastly remains of even living bodies, can have no conception of the word 'danger' – and even the word 'risk.' You in the US are like we were when we heard first of the Japanese bombing of China. We felt it was awful, but it did not touch us, we could not understand. Then Poland got it and somehow it felt still more awful. We were distressed and subscribed willingly to relief funds. We felt something ought to be done about it, but still it did not touch us and we still did not understand. But all Britain fully understands now.

I gather that even Mrs. Roosevelt has been considerably staggered at what she has seen of the bomb damage. But even she cannot see the damage and wreckage of human lives and the maimed in body and mind. To realize it you have to experience it. For the rest of my life when I hear of horrors, I shall always feel they must be so much worse than anything that I can imagine. Aerial warfare has taught me that much. Of course there is a risk of submarine and air attack crossing the Atlantic, but many thousands of folk do get across each way quite safely.

November 2, 1942

I have just come back from seeing 'Young Mr. Pitt' on the films. It was just great and just right to hear English actors and not US in an English historical film. Talk about history repeating itself! The arrangement about invasion by Napoleon was accompanied by gunfire which made it all so modern. A young sailor sitting in front of me actually saluted when Admiral Lord Nelson came on the screen! I was very amused. The quaint old wooden ships of those days would be mighty little use in these days. But it all was so like present day happenings. It might almost have been Mr. Churchill instead of Mr. Pitt only of course there were no air raids. They also showed a film of Mrs. Roosevelt visiting all our war organizations. She spoke through the microphone to a company of women workers. A great lady from a great land. She is winning her way to British hearts by her friendliness and interest in every thing she is shown. Her visit will do a great deal of good.

Here are some of the uses of herbs you ask about: Spearmint, a flavor of mint used in mint sauce. Rue for bilious attacks and indigestion. Feverfew, to reduce feverishness. Southernwood or Lad's Love dried for sweet smelling concoctions, medicine, and moths. Rosemary many uses, very fragrant. Bay for flavoring puddings, would do for meats. White Satter, I think is meant for homes, etc., is used for winter decorations. Lavender cotton for moths and medicine. Lavender for fragrance, sugar rosets and medicine. Penny Royal, medicine. Smalledge or Smallage in cooking. Ale Hoof to flavor home brewed ale. Gilly flowers, fragrance and syrups. Fennel for sauce served chiefly with fish. Horseleek (Houseleek) for ointment.

I am treating myself to Noel Coward's 'Blithe Spirit' next week. I understand it is very good.

By what Mrs. Roosevelt says women are not much organized in US for war work.

November 5, 1942

9 Edale Road, Sheffield, England

Today I had the pleasure of going out to lunch with a young engineer soldier home on leave. To assure you that we have plenty of food, here was our choice from next to the lowest priced menu (there were two higher than that) at a nice but not outrageously expensive cafe: brown onion soup (with real onion in it in spite of the shortage), saute kidney, mashed turnips, roasted or mashed potatoes. He had fruit tart custard and I had raspberry mold with synthetic cream, and we both had coffee. It was well cooked, and no coupons had to be given up. We thoroughly enjoyed it.

After finishing my shopping, he escorted me to my bus and I came home only to find that the air raid sirens had sounded. From the demeanor of the public no one would have known that anything was about. It is difficult to hear planes and sirens above the roar of traffic, and at first I wondered why there were so many firemen and police about!

Otherwise all went their normal ways. Our supply of bread was delivered during gunfire and the only comment made by the old man delivering it was, 'I hope they get the devils!' I sat and added substantially to my knitting by a nice warm fire. When the performance was over two friends came in to tea and we had quite a good time.

Yesterday I met someone I have known all my life. She had lived in a beautiful home surrounded by china and furniture handed down for generations, but she told me she lost everything in the blitz – not as much as a cup handle left! However, she seemed as cheerful as ever and there was no grumbling.

Winston Churchill came to Sheffield last week and had a tremendous welcome, quite a royal welcome in fact with scenes of tremendous enthusiasm everywhere. He got quite excited himself. He has a boyish expression behind that grim bulldog look of his when he smiles and laughs. Because of German bombers, his arrival here was kept a close secret until he was actually in the city.

I am off to our reference library to do some research related to my work. Most of the libraries I used to know have been called up, so it is difficult to find the books I want. Most of them are several hundred years old and as so few people need them, they have been put in hiding.

I am volunteering for sorting work at the post office. Some of the university students have also volunteered. I like working with young people. It will be a way of helping as most of the men have been called up and it will be a new experience to be added to life. I only hope I shan't have to rise at some unearthly hour in the morning to do it.

During a recent raid a man was having a bath and a blast from a bomb blew the tub complete with sponge and man to the far side of a field near his home. I trust he was not arrested for being indecently clad when he ran back to the remains of his house. This incident is always being held up to me now as an awful warning not to have a bath after blackout!

It disgusts me to read of the strikes in your country. I wonder if many of the strikers are not being influenced by German propaganda. If only they knew the real Nazis, but they would have to sit through one of our nine-hour blitzes to do that, and thousands of miles away it is so easy to be indifferent to the urgency of things. I don't want America to have any, but I wish the strikers might come over here and sit through not just a raid, but a real blitz. There would be no thought of strikes left then.

Mr. G., where I am now living, is an air raid warden. At the post he has to contact, there is another warden whose dog (a spaniel) insists on following him. He leaves her outside, but after a few minutes she pushes the door open and walks into the post. Whereupon the doorkeeper invariably records her visit in the attendance book 'name, Cissie Outran; time, 19.23'. (They use army time in warden's post.) Can you imagine a German or Italian post doing anything like that? Their cruelty and brutality would crush all sense of humor. It must be horrible to have all fun and frivolity suppressed for fear of offending the Nazis. I should have been in a concentration camp or shot long ago if I had been in a Nazi governed country, for I can't help laughing at amusing things. The French and Italians seem more human, and how they must hate their German bosses. Still, it is their own fault for pandering to the beasts.

NOTE: *On 8 November 1942, US and British troops made an amphibious landing on the coast of French North Africa. Called Operation Torch, it was the first time large numbers of American troops saw action in the war against Germany.*

November 8, 1942

I have just heard that US troops have landed in North Africa. It was announced over the air at 2:30 a.m. We are all very thrilled and feel that at last the US is really fighting! We are all quite excited.

People's query: 'What are American soldiers doing?' will be answered now. We know your air force has helped, but your soldiers did not seem to be doing much fighting. That will be a nasty blow for Hitler and company. I am wondering if they will go to Russia. I know nothing at all about strategy, and always feel that in spite of their mistakes our leaders know so much more than any of us that we can safely leave everything to them without worrying as to how, why, when or where! Though it is only natural to wonder occasionally.

I wonder too, if Mrs. Roosevelt will fly to North Africa to see your troops. I'm certain she has the pluck to do it. She has made a great impression over here and I am sure that her visit will do a great deal of good. She came at a time when some gesture of friendliness was very welcome. We keep hearing about anti–British feeling in the States. Personally I think it is the work of fifth columnists and US isolationists. There is bound to be such talk in a country the size of US.

November 9, 1942

Everyone is delighted to hear that Algiers has surrendered to the US troops – another nasty knock for Hitler's mob. We have collared

Madagascar, and no doubt Morocco will succumb to the Allies before so long. Enough to make that detestable snake Laval writhe in rage and despair.

I must say that it gave me somewhat of a nasty shock to see the Hammer and Sickle floating with the very lovable Union Jack, the cheerful encouraging Stars and Stripes and the pathetic Free French flags over our Town Hall this morning. The Hammer and Sickle had got itself in a muddle around the flagstaff!

We all listened to Mrs. Roosevelt last evening. She spoke very well indeed. She has very little accent too. I guess the US forces were glad to see her when she visited them.

I have been to six shops to try to get some bezique cards – they are not obtainable. So disappointing. Two of us in the boarding house want to play bezique in the evening occasionally.

I forget whether I told you I had been to see 'Young Mr. Pitt' and 'Mrs. Minniver' on the films. Both are very good. The former might stand for today and the latter is a very amusing yet pathetic picture of English home life in war time. Do go to see them.

November 10, 1942

The news continues to be good. Good enough to impress Hitler so much that he publicly states that 'it does not make much difference.' I'm afraid he will find it will make a difference. I should think the Recording Angel has filled many volumes with the lies Hitler has told. A special celestial library will be needed to record his evil deeds and lies!!

> **NOTE:** On 11 November 1942 there was a major British victory over General Rommel's forces at El Alamein in Egypt. That combined with the American landing in North Africa and the Russian siege at Stalingrad gave a badly needed lift to the Allied cause.

November 15, 1942

Today we have had a victory celebration on account of the Germans being on the run in North Africa. I personally did not approve of the church bells being rung, as they were not to be rung except in the case of invasion, and any one who had not heard the statement on the wireless, might easily be scared into thinking that we were invaded at last! I think we should have waited till the enemy was out of North Africa altogether, however, the authorities thought otherwise – otherwise it was! I should think Hitler and company are feeling anxious just now.

The government has announced that one in five houses in Britain have been damaged by bombs, exclusive of windows blown but minor damage such as doors, chimneys and parts of roofs. This does not include shops, offices, and public buildings such as churches, halls, art galleries, etc. One in a thousand have been repaired, not many is it? That ought to arouse some of the apathetic Americans who even yet don't realize what we are up against. Try to picture England and remember that even yet there are many places untouched by bombs so that you can guess the interests of the raids and the state of the big cities that have suffered.

A little while ago I visited a paper salvage place where the waste paper was sorted, repulped, and made into such a variety of things that I should never have thought possible. It gives me added satisfaction every time I empty my waste paper into the salvage sack to think that some German will get something he doesn't like from some letter I have liked!!

November 23, 1942

What a week of good news! The other p.m. some of us listened to Haw Haw's successor. It purported to be from the workers of the Soviet Union to the British workers. The silly donkeys (really Germans are fools) hadn't the sense to realize that no Soviet members would, at the present time, refer to 'Bloody Roosevelt and Churchill' or call either of them B------s. The language was fearfully lurid and the whole talk was deliberately planned to stir up trouble between us and the Soviet Union.

Mrs. Roosevelt is now safe at home in her own country. She told us that one of the things that struck her worst was the 'utter blackout of Britain'. Apparently your blackouts are far from 'utter' and unless you have ever groped about in darkness that can literally be felt, you can have no idea what it is like and the dangers thereof in big cities. I think all things considered we have remarkably few accidents in the blackout.

Owing to the fuel shortage there are no buses run after 9 p.m. except for the workers. All theatres, cinemas, and other places of amusement have to close before then to allow patrons to get away before the last bus. How would you like that in USA? It cuts everyone off entirely who lives on a bus route, where there is no train service also. Of course private cars disappeared long ago. Everyone has turned the whole thing into a joke and accepts the ruling without a murmur. I think it will lead to the restoration of family life, hard work, and parlor games again. Even in the BH they are settling down with enthusiasm to chess, solo, cribbage, etc. I badly want to play bezique, a really good card game for two. Do you know it? I have been all over Sheffield trying to get a set of bezique cards and the markers. They are absolutely unobtainable.

The shops close at 4 p.m. if they have any thing to sell or not. Life is not very frisky at present in England but it sounds more lively in Italy, Libya, and Stalingrad at present. I should think Hitler must surely be feeling very uncomfortable inside. Even as I also am feeling for tomorrow I begin at the Man Power Board office filling in forms for ten hours a day, and five on Saturdays. Just think of it, ten hours a day sitting at a desk with eighty other people, all ages, sizes, and shapes doing nothing but the same thing over and over again except for the name. I have taken it on temporarily till I leave for the States. It is war work and they badly need help. It is so terribly monotonous and such long hours that many find they can't stick it for long. I wonder if I shall be able to stick with it. I have not been used to being pinned down. If I had to write for long at home I could always leave my desk for a few minutes to take a breather in my garden. There was always something to refresh one's mind and body there. But at the MPB I shall not be able to do that, but shall have to keep on keeping on. I believe that one can always do what one has to do, so hope to live up to the belief once more.

CONCLUSION

I wish I had more of a denouement to offer. We all know how the war turned out. As for Winifred Graville, despite months of anticipation and preparation, including selling her house, she apparently never went to the United States for her lecture tour. She most certainly would have visited her American cousin, but there was no mention in the local newspaper of her coming to Penn Yan after the war. After publishing 150 of her letters, there certainly would have been some mention of it in the *Chronicle-Express*.

One has to assume that she continued with her intense interest in gardening. She lived out the remainder of her life in Sheffield, dying there in September of 1974 at the age of 89. The two transatlantic cousins' letter-writing campaign of 1939–42 had no impact whatsoever at getting the USA to ally with Britain against Nazi Germany, but the letters have left us with a remarkable and deeply personal account of the spirit and pluck of the British people during a fearful time in history.

ABOUT THE EDITOR

Richard MacAlpine retired from a thirty-four year career of teaching American and European History at a high school in Oneida, New York in 2001. Upon retirement, he and his wife moved to a home in Yates County in the Finger Lakes region. There he pursued his passion of researching and writing about family history, which evolved into an interest in the local history of his area. He became active in the Yates County History Center in Penn Yan, New York, and became the editor and chief writer for their bimonthly publication, *Yates Past*. He has researched and written over 150 articles for them about various aspects of local history. Several of those stories have worked their way into two books: *Yates County Chronicles* (The History Press USA, 2014) and *Stories From Yates Past* (Infinity Publishing, 2016).

As well as his articles, Richard has written *Steamboats on Keuka Lake: Penn Yan, Hammondsport and the Heart of the Finger Lakes* (co-authored with Charles R. Mitchell, The History Press USA, 2015), *Admiral Frank H. Schofield: A Portrait in Letters of An American Navy Family (1886–1942)* (Infinity Publishing, 2016) and *'Over There' and Over Here: Yates County in the Great War (1916–1919)* (Infinity Publishing, 2018).

Richard and his wife Jeanie have a home on Keuka Lake, just outside Penn Yan. They raised three children while in Oneida and now have nine grandchildren.

IF YOU ENJOYED THIS TITLE FROM THE HISTORY PRESS

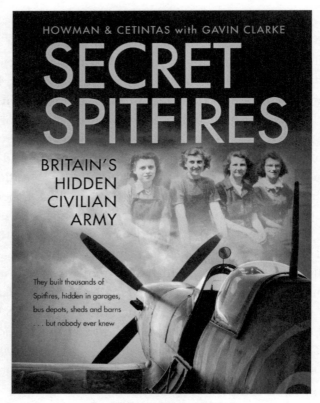

978 0 7509 9199 5

PENNY STARNS

BLITZ HOSPITAL

TRUE STORIES OF NURSING
IN WARTIME LONDON

978 0 7509 8249 8

The History Press
The destination for history
www.thehistorypress.co.uk